# MUSIC LEGENDS

## A Rewind on the Minnesota Music Scene

By Martin Keller

the *Minnesota* series

Prince performing in the rain at the 2007 Superbowl in Miami. Prince, Flyte Time and their impact on the Minnesota music scene will be featured in *Music Legends 2*.
[photo: Associated Press]

# Welcome to Music Legends

**M**usic Legends is the second book in The Minnesota Series. Inside you'll find stories and pictures that chronicle the Minnesota music scene from the 1950s and beyond. This is one of two Music Legends books in the series. Each book will inform, entertain and feature stories and pictures about the known and the "not so known."

Past and coming books in The Minnesota Series include: *Storms!*, *Media Tales* (our next title), *Storms 2*, *Sports Legends*, *Famous Crimes*, *Politics*, *Newsmakers*, *Urban Legends* and more. A companion CD to Music Legends featuring Minnesota music is also in development. Books are available at retailers statewide and at minnesotaseries.com. We invite you to collect and enjoy all the books in the series!

Author **Martin Keller**
Editor **Sheri O'Meara**
Design and Layout **Phil Tippin**
Web Consultant **Risdall Advertising, New Brighton, Minn.**
Printing **Bang Printing, Brainerd, Minn.**
Publishing and Production Management **Jim Bindas, Books & Projects LLC**
Transportation **Maplewood Toyota**
Publishers **D Media: Debra Gustafson Decker, Dale Decker**

©2007 by D Media Inc., 4601 Excelsior Blvd #301, Minneapolis, Minn. 55416.
(952) 926-3950. dmedia@juno.com. www.minnesotaseries.com.
Subscriptions available at www.minnesotaseries.com

ISBN 978-0-9787956-1-0

*Library of Congress Control Number 2006938771*

# Contents

On the Cover: Bob Dylan (photo: courtesy Columbia Records),
Yanni (photo: Associated Press), The Replacements (photo: Greg Helgeson).

# Foreword

Minnesota offered a lot to a kid from western North Dakota, who arrived for college in the lakes state with a trunk full of records, a few clothes and some half-cocked dreams to write about music one day. Many years, news clips and backstage passes later, the unusual opportunity presented itself yet again with this book about the storied Minnesota music scene.

Having jumped to the other side of the desk to do public relations as part of a self-diagnosed mid-life crisis many more years ago, I got to know various musicians you'll read about here even better as artists and entertainers, and as people.

Is the book complete? Not by a long shot. Another music book, an encore to bring us forward from the '80s, is on the docket in The Minnesota Series. Did some bands, players and singers get left out in this one? Regrettably, the band-stand (and the editor's word count per chapter) only holds so many. Hopefully, the stories of those told here will give you as much satisfaction as the records they made, the scenes they created and the lives they shared with us all through their unforgettable work. ♪

**Martin Keller**

The High Spirits: One of Soma Records' many young rock artists, with Owen Husney (lower left), who later worked with Prince.
(photo: courtesy Timothy D. Kehr Collection)

# The Dawn of Minnesota Rock and Roll
## *The 1950s, '60s and Soma Records*

The day Garcia died in 1995, Minneapolis comedian, actor and Pepito's restaurateur Joe Minjares first thought *Augie* Garcia had kicked, not Jerry Garcia of the Grateful Dead. While many may not know Augie, let alone remember him, the West side St. Paul native, whose heyday was from the mid-'50s to mid-'60s, has often been dubbed the godfather of Minnesota rock 'n' roll. According to the Minnesota Historical Society, Augie also had the distinction of opening (kind of) for Elvis Presley in '56 at the St. Paul Auditorium and of always wearing Bermuda shorts.

The society's notes on Garcia reveal that "...his high-energy show in his trademark Bermuda shorts was too much for Presley's manager, Col. Tom Parker. The crowd became frenzied, Garcia later recalled, and Parker pulled him from the stage, citing a clause in Garcia's contract that barred competition with the headliner. The shorts were a Garcia trademark. He recalled that he had 38 pairs of them that he wore in both summer and winter." And so, more or less, Minnesota's earliest rock scene was born on a loopy fashion statement and a swift boot out of the court of the colonel and the King.

Garcia and his dubiously (re)named band, the Augie Garcia Quintet, had one major area hit in '65 with "Hi Yo Silver" on the North Star imprint. But by then – after obscure rockabilly groups, horn bands and others cutting tracks on even more obscure labels and playing wherever they could – Minnesota's rock soil had been plowed and planted by pioneers like Garcia and (according to *Lost and Found*, a '50s and '60s 'zine) by The Velquins, The Delricos, The Flames and others in the late-'50s who all cut sides for one of the small independent labels of the day, Gaity Records.

As the '60s dawned, The Fabulous Jades and the improbably named Yetti-Men, who hailed from Minnetonka, briefly lit up dance halls like The Prom, area high schools, sock hops, private parties, night spots and various Battles of the Bands. And by the time astronaut John Glen had zipped around the earth three times in a space capsule, Minnesota's first rock harvest was slowly beginning to roll in, as greasy kid stuff hairdos captured in landmark films like *American Graffiti* morphed into mop tops, then the long, psychedelic tresses of late-'60s.

The scene that sprang up prior to and after the 1964 British invasion produced some of the earliest national hits from the land of 10,000 lakes and dances. But it also contained (within the groups, recording studios and offices that made and booked the music) many key people that formed the foundation and early infrastructure of the Minnesota music business. These individuals and establishments would come to fruition over the next two decades, making the Twin Cities a more viable music center and lessening the need for musicians to move to Los Angeles or Manhattan.

One could never capture the adolescent trappings of that period, the rapture fans felt seeing those early live rock shows or the blizzard of bands. But essential collections like *The Big Hits of Mid-America: The Soma Records Story 1963-1967* (Plum Records) say it all, frequently in twangin'-surf-guitar-and-Farfisa-organ glory. With insightful liner notes by Jordan, Minn., resident and fan Jim Oldsberg, the two-disc set readily provides an engrossing soundtrack to the liberating night sounds.

You could hear them live at Big Reggie's Danceland in Excelsior, or along University Avenue near Pudge's and on Lake Street as kids dragged up and down the strips blaring their radios set to WDGY and KDWB and polishing their cool, while bopping to bands on the Soma Records label such as Gregory Dee and the Avantis and others. While Soma Records had the inside track on the music business then, many '60s bands recorded for other independent labels, including Danny's Reasons (led by the flamboyant Danny Stevens – aka Capri), whose work later showed up on the extensive *Pebbles Collections*. Like many of his peers, Stevens would also go on to play a commercial role in the fledging music business. He helped to open The Depot, which ultimately became First Avenue.

The Twin Cities scene that spawned the earliest big hits also produced its share of insiders, movers and shakers like Stevens. Among them were booking agents such as Dick Shapiro (who later formed Company 7 and, like his later competitor, Randy Levy at Schon Productions, brought many major acts to the Twin Cities for years). Bill Diehl was simultaneously a WDGY jock and *Pioneer Press* news guy. Ray Colihan (aka "Big Reggie) ran Danceland. He was a tall, friendly man who stayed in the business well into an advancing age at the

Uptown Bar in the '80s and unabashedly boasted of being the only man in the world to lose money on both The Beatles and the Rolling Stones.

The Fab Four rocked Met Stadium in August 1965 but did not sell out. The Stones on their first U.S. tour at Danceland reportedly played rather sloppily to 300 or so fans who showed up in June of '64, who frequently booed them throughout the set. Urban legend has it that it was there the next day at a local Excelsior drugstore, with a certain local figure, Mr. Jimmy, that Mick Jagger got the inspiration for "You Can't Always Get What You Want" (or at least the line). That notion has been debunked online. Still, the story refuses to die. As recently as July 2006, the local *Lakeshore Weekly News* ran yet another account of the tale and an interview with Mr. Jimmy.

For much of that nascent rock 'n' roll era in Minnesota, Soma Records' output of 45 rpm records ramped up the action. As early as 1959, its prescient founders Amos Heilicher and partner Vern Bank were already hitting the charts with a young Bobby Vee and the Shadows' tune, "Suzy Baby," after buying a simple studio at 25th and Nicollet Avenue South and renaming it Kay Bank Studios (after Bank's wife). Kay Bank would become a monumental fixture in the history of Minnesota music, later becoming Cookhouse Studios and one home of Twin/Tone Records. Countless musicians from all styles of popular music, from jazz to country, have recorded there.

Flying on the strengths of his first single, Vee would soon go on to California to become one of rock's "teen idols." According to Oldsberg, other labels like North Star, Hep, Oxboro, Gaity, Bear Records/Lieberman Brothers competed with Soma for the sounds of the era, but Soma rocked the region and dominated the business. Heilicher, who occasionally personally recorded old-time music like polka bands prior to the '60s, also had a pressing plant in town and had been in the music business with his brother Daniel since the '40s. Prior to Soma, working as Heilicher Brothers, the two visionary businessmen were already immersed nationally in the jukebox distribution side and other facets of the early music industry.

Although they were land-locked in the middle of the country away from the coasts of LA and New York where much of the industry was well-established, ironically, the Heilichers were already among the earliest giants in the biz as the '60s rolled out. *Esquire* magazine named Amos one of the industry's Top 100 people during that period. Soon the brothers would become major retailers, too: In 1964, they opened the national Musicland franchise, with 126 stores nationwide eventually, and merged Heilicher Brothers with Pickwick International Inc. in 1977.

Their early "rack jobbing" (stocking and tracking records) business was formidable enough. But once Amos moved things into the creative end – where regional indie vinyl met the national supply chain in a beautiful Midwest marriage of art and commerce – the Twin Cities music scene beamed onto America's cultural radar, even though it was only rock 'n'roll.

Many groups from the early era copied lesser-known African-American R&B bands, or the lads from Liverpool and other Top of the Pops places in the UK.

But some of the teen hitmakers at Soma (Amos spelled backwards, and not the dreamy drug of Aldous Huxley's *Brave New World* novel) really did have a signature style and lasting effect. The Trashmen's "Surfin' Bird" (climbing to #4 on Billboard's Hot 100, only to be blown out by George, Paul, John and Ringo) was an instant garage rock classic that served as a loud-fast muse for the Ramones and many others 15 years later in the new wave period. But the principals at Soma and Kay Bank took a somewhat dimmer, and/or ironic, view of that particular 45 rpm disc.

"The Bird is the worst I've ever heard," Bank wrote to Amos on the sleeve of an early copy of the record that first was on Garrett Records before Soma picked it up. "Must be a hit. Call me if you're interested." Perhaps Bank's message was really tongue-in-cheek, since he partially quoted the song's lyrics. Amos, who turned 89 in November 2006, recalls convincing his "radio buddies in the Twin Cities" to play "Surfin' Bird" and other sides that he cut. The first day in the stores The Bird sold out its initial pressing of 1,000 copies. Then it sold 10,000 copies as it got added to playlists in the region. Sensing a hit, Amos sent it to his distribution colleagues at Mercury Records, "about 30 guys around the country," again with the caveat (or a wink and a nudge) in a handwritten note that said, "It's a terrible record. See if you like it." Over 1 million copies later, America's teenagers – and lots of DJs – had voted: They loved it!

Heilicher had a knack for breaking other cool records. Besides talented kids coming into record with their bands as long as they could afford the studio time, Amos often helped

promote their work by "going up to the local radio stations
at night with a six pack and some pizzas" and new copies of
songs that Soma had recorded. "Play this a few times tonight,"
I told them. "You could do that back then," he laughs, "the
early business was like that." Was that his form of payola
– pizzaola? "The only payola I ever did was take some record
execs out on a boat for dinner on Minnetonka once," chuckles
the godfather of the Minnesota music business.

Pizza or not, Soma Records' bands often made the
grade, producing records that withstood the test of time and
creating more opportunities for local musicians. The Castaways' immortal 1965 hit "Liar Liar" ended up in the prestigious *Nuggets Collection* in the '70s. The Underbeats, led by
Jim Johnson, recorded a number of important singles but
later would evolve into the renowned late-'60s band Gypsy,
with James Walsh. Mankato's finest, The Gestures, produced
one of the most deftly "composed" original hits of the time,
"Never Mess Around," written by Dale Menten. The group
even scored on America's other "really big shew," Dick Clark's
*American Bandstand* show. Later, Menten went on to run Cookhouse. Today he operates downtown, working frequently in
the commercial world of advertising and sound design, with a
few peculiar ventures into film production.

Besides delivering their share of local hits, The High
Spirits and The Chancellors (also Soma recording stars) gave
us Owen Husney from the Spirits and David Rivkin, who
played in both combos. Husney took up management of a
young kid named Prince Rogers Nelson in the late-'70s, while
Rivkin ended up producing him for a time under the name

David Z, along with Jonny Lang, Kenny Wayne Shepherd, Fine Young Cannibals and others. Rivkin also engineered the biggest hit from Mid-America, "Funkytown."

The revolution that rock 'n' roll fueled here and across American culture firmly took root in the early-'60s. But by 1970, the music was forever changed as the country slid into darker times with the war in Vietnam, the civil rights struggle, environmental and women's rights issues, plus the debilitating political assassinations of the Kennedys, Malcom X and Martin Luther King. But for a brief, fleeting time, transistor radios, hi-fi's stacked with 45s and black-and-white TV sets infiltrated the airwaves with the sounds from the bandstands and two-track recording studios that romantically launched an era of high hopes and rock 'n' roll dreams.

"It was a fun time, a fun time," says Amos Heilicher today, some 40 years later. You can go there again by dropping a Soma tune into your home theater system, your iPod or your memory. ♪

The Castaways' classic hit "Liar Liar" has withstood the test of time on disc and on movie soundtracks.
(photo: courtesy Timothy D. Kehr Collection)

The Underbeats: Later morphing into Gypsy and featuring Jim Johnson and Jim Walsh.
(photo: courtesy Timothy D. Kehr Collection)

Danny Stevens (center) was an early shaker in Danny's Reasons but also was a major mover later in opening The Depot (now First Avenue).
(photo: courtesy Timothy D. Kehr Collection)

The Trashmen, who recorded the often-covered "Surfin Bird'," pictured here in the '60s left to right: Steve Wahrer, Bob Reed, Tony Andreason and Dal Winslow.
(photo: courtesy Timothy D. Kehr Collection)

The Chancellors pictured here at the U of M in the '60s.
(photo: courtesy Timothy D. Kehr Collection)

Amos (left) and Daniel Heilicher: Visionary businessmen who married Midwest rock 'n' roll and
commerce with Soma Records and the retail chain first called Musicland.
(photo: Earl Seubert, January 21, 1969)

# Minnesota's Great Singers

The honor guard stood silently while a couple hundred people gathered around the site at Lakewood Cemetery in south Minneapolis and listened in awe to the singer during a special Memorial Day tribute. As his transcendent voice soared, filling the fresh spring air with "America the Beautiful," tears welled up in the eyes of many gathered among the silent tombstones. It doesn't matter where gospel and pop singer Robert Robinson sings – gravesites, churches, with Prince or Aretha Franklin, or onstage with Lorie Line in her annual Christmas pageant. When Robinson sings, emotions stir and hearts lift.

Minnesota has produced a profound assortment of gifted vocalists not in the rock, folk and jazz realms like classical music singer Maria Jette, Broadway star and Minnesota native Linda Eder, plus the fine casts of numerous singers that nightly populate the dinner theaters and the scores of theatrical stages throughout the state. But with the well-defined talents and careers of Robinson, The Sounds of Blackness and The Blenders, special props must be given for the magic they've created through the years and the joy that they've given to the thousands who've seen them in concert or heard them on record.

Often described as the "Pavarotti of Gospel," Robinson is first and foremost a gospel powerhouse, singing the African-American Christian music of this country that in its earliest form seeded the roots of R&B, jazz and rock 'n'

Robert Robinson in concert stirs the deep emotions.
(photo: courtesy Robert Robinson)

roll. But the sensitivity and majesty he brings to any song, whether it's "Wonderous Day of Our God" or the 1960s pop hit "Higher and Higher" by Jackie Wilson, his singing is as distinctive as the elegant design and stunning color of a Bird of Paradise flower.

For a time Robinson would sing only the Lord's music. But as he's gotten older, the singer has embraced secular music "as long as the music has a message and a positive direction," according to writer Michael Reinbold, recollecting a stirring performance Robinson gave at his CD release party at St. Joan of Arc Church in South Minneapolis. Robinson has been singing – and literally leading other gospel singers including the other Robinson siblings in a family group called The Robinson Children – since he was 6 years old.

Today he is the executive artistic director of the 110-member Twin Cities Community Gospel Choir, and his voice is featured on various album projects with one of the area's beacons of the gospel music scene, Sam Davis and his Gospel Ensemble. Robinson has also sung live and on record with Minneapolis Gospel Sound, GT and the Halo Express, Volume 10, Connell Lewis and the Cornerstone and Excelsior Choral Ensemble. But it's his own records and those made with Lorie Line that truly shine, although he parted company with Line recently.

According to his web site biography (www.robertrobinsonmusic.com), In the summer of 2001 Lorie Line produced a solo project for Robert entitled *The Show Stoppers*, then a culmination of the work they'd done together for 13 years. To date, his seven solo projects (including *From the Heart, From the Heart Vol. 2, Christmas From the Heart,*

*Praise From the Heart, The Show Stoppers* and his most recent
releases, *Robert Robinson "Live" with Friends, Songs for the
Season and Inspiration*) demonstrate the depth of his vocal
talent and the refined sensibility behind it. He has also
produced three projects through Compass Productions that
are distributed exclusively through Target Stores: *Gospel
Hymns, Gospel Christmas* and *Amazing Grace*.

The man who was voted "2004 Best Gospel Artist"
by the Minnesota Music Academy can truly transform any
space with his blessed abilities. An October 1991 Theater
de la Jeune Lune production of *The Nightingale*, in which
he played the lead role, ran for almost four months and
was the second-highest attended show in the company's
rich history. Robinson is a rare bird indeed – and one of
Minnesota's musical treasures.

Although they have the divine power and hard
numbers of a great gospel choir, The Grammy-Award-
winning Sounds of Blackness have earned most of their
glory in the dance and pop world under the direction of the
ever-buff (former) Mr. Minnesota, Gary Hines. According
to the web site Discogs, "Russel Knight formed the group
that would prove to be the origins of Sounds of Blackness in
1969 at Macalester College." But it was Hines who eventually took them over the moon when he became the director
of the 30- to 40-member group of singers and instrumentalists in 1971. These three-time Grammy champions and
winners of numerous other awards collectively feature an
ensemble sound that is as heavenly as it is firmly rooted
"on the street." Their musical embrace touches on reggae,

ragtime, field hollers, R&B, jazz – you name it – the Sounds can sing it!

The group discovered a stunning "souloist" in Ann Bennett Nesby. She went on to enjoy a rich solo career with three No. 1 R&B singles from her first solo project, *I'm Here For You*, produced by the powerhouse duo of Jimmy Jam and Terry Lewis. She scored top-five hits on *Billboard's* Hot Dance Music/Club Play charts and had a role in the film *The Fighting Temptations*. She also has three Grammy nominations, including in 2002 for Best Traditional R&B Vocal Performance ("Put It On Paper," featuring Al Green); in 2003 for Best Contemporary Soul Gospel Album (*Make Me Better*); and a 2004 nomination for Best Gospel Performance (for "The Stone" featuring Shirley Caesar from *The Fighting Temptations* soundtrack). Bennett Nesby also has the distinction of being the fawning grandmother of 2006 *American Idol* finalist Paris Bennett, who finished in the top five in 2006.

Producers Jimmy Jam and Terry Lewis (who would later produce three albums for them) were instrumental in getting the Sounds of Blackness signed to a major label when the producers took Janet Jackson to see the ensemble. She flipped for them. Today, with eight records to their credit, this big entourage has lived up to its mission of illuminating the many gifts of African-American culture in the wider world and on Broadway with a Christmas show, based on their 1993 Perspective/A&M album *The Night Before Christmas – A Musical Fantasy*.

Through the strength of their vocal power and vision, they've become goodwill musical ambassadors, too, performing three times for audiences of over 1 billion people at the Opening Ceremonies of the 1994 World Cup, the 1996 Summer Olympics and the 1998 World Figure Skating Championships. The group has also performed at the White House five times. But no matter where they go, the Sounds of Blackness will always elicit shouts of "Amen" and "Oh Yeah!"

Not so far removed from the Sounds, or Robinson, are Fargo natives The Blenders, who have made the Twin Cities their home for more than a dozen years after establishing themselves as one of the most creative and innovative forces in the a cappella world, mixing jazz, barber shop, doo wop, R&B, gospel, rock and a cappella styles together. The self-described "vocal band" consists of Tim Kasper and Ryan Lance (two life-long friends from the age of 5) and the brothers Allan and Darren Rust (who grew up on a farm outside of what Kasper likes to call "that Academy Award-winning town of Fargo"). They were in many ways pathfinders in the a cappella music world, and a bridge into pop for a cappella singers.

"The Blenders were in the vanguard of contemporary vocal bands when I started the first a cappella catalog in 1992," says Don Gooding, founder and president of the Mainely A Cappella family of companies (headquartered in Maine) that offers the largest selection of a cappella music in the world. "They were one of a small number of guy groups doing a mix of fantastic original material along with covers, and their sound is unique in several respects. They were able to rock with no vocal percussion while emphasizing harmonic blend to an extent mostly found in vocal jazz groups like The Singers Unlimited."

Since they stopped touring and striving to be a "boy band" in the early -'90s when briefly signed to Universal Records, The Blenders' record and perform now only for the holidays (with some corporate gigs during the year), occasionally reprising their pop material live in between the Christmas chestnuts, with tunes such as "Loveland" or "(I'm in Love With) The McDonald's Girl," which was a hit for them in Scandinavia and New Zealand!

"As their careers progressed they added instrumentation at times," Gooding explains, "as did Take 6, out of both artistic vision and commercial pressure. During an era in which boy bands attempted to sing a cappella to show off their chops, these guys could do it in their sleep. It's unfortunate that the music industry never understood them, but that's been pretty typical for a cappella vocal bands over the last 15 years."

Misunderstood or not, The Blenders have toured with Jay Leno, Howie Mandell and others and been on *The Today Show*, Arsenio Hall, CNN, National Public Radio and other programs. And anyone who's seen them live at their Christmas concerts, checked out their four Christmas CDs, or heard any of their densely layered pop albums, including the feel-good collection of covers (recorded with a hot Nashville sessions band) called *Songs from the Soul* that they released for the 2006 holidays, knows that the term vocal band is an apt description. Darren Rust's alchemical production mixes in both the recording studio and live onstage often feature five-and six-part a cappella harmonies and instruments that are often really the singers' voices.

"Over time, Darren Rust's production prowess grew enormously," Gooding notes. "*Nog* (their first Christmas album in 1997) was truly a breakthrough for the group, and made Darren a sought-after producer in the vocal harmony community. His take on achieving a cappella perfection in the studio differs from other big name a cappella producers – again, the emphasis on lush harmonic blend and the absence of vocal distortion effects commonly used in more rock-oriented a cappella production."

Through nine ho-ho-ho years now, audiences from 1 to 93 have made The Blender's holiday shows throughout the region a tradition, lapping up the group's *The Mighty Wind* folk parody where they appear as The Folkers, or their hilarious sendup as a country gospel show in Branson starring The Krumplers. But it's their sophisticated arrangements of standard carols and hymns, a few tricked-out Christmas standards and their own endearing seasonal songs, plus the moving solos sung by Allan and the guys throughout the performance that keep people coming back.

The singers' doo-wop driven "Tiny Little Christmas," the retro disco vamp of "All Wrapped Up" and the warm R&B ballad and title of their second holiday disc, *When It Snows* (which international R&B and pop diva Erykah Badu named as her favorite Christmas record in 2002 in the *Dallas Morning News*), were written by Lance. When he is isn't playing Santa's little songsmith, he sings in a fun '80s group with his wife, Heidi Jo Langseth (the sister of Jonny Lang) called Brat Pack Radio. But just how influential have they been?

Gooding says that The Blenders' arrangements have filtered into the a cappella world through "both official and unofficial channels." Their original work was published, and more recently their holiday arrangements have become available through sheet music giant Hal Leonard Corp. "Numerous groups have transcribed their arrangements over the years, a traditional – if questionably legal – way of paying homage to influential a cappella groups," Gooding says. Santa will note that on his list. The versatile vocal band from Fargo remains a major influence on a new generation vocal singers including Tonic Sol Fa and others. The Blenders have given Minnesotans – and the world – the gift of smart and enduring a cappella music that sounds good any time of the year. ♪

#### Chapter 2

Until 2006, Robert Robinson (at microphone) was a featured performer in the
annual Lorie Line Christmas extravaganza.
(photo: Associated Press)

Sounds of Blackness celebrates African-American culture in all of its musical genres from the pop charts and Broadway to the rest of the world.
(photo: courtesy of The Sounds of Blackness)

Powerful Flyte Tyme producers Jimmy Jam and Terry Lewis produced The Sounds of Blackness'
debut album, after taking Janet Jackson to see the ensemble in concert,
where she became an instant fan.
(photo: Associated Press)

The Blenders: Giants of the a cappella music world who successfully moved to pop as
a "vocal band," originally from "the Academy Award winning town of Fargo."
(photo: courtesy of The Blenders)

# Famous Families of Minnesota Music

Y ou've heard the old adage how Minnesota is a great place
to raise kids? It's also been a great place for Minnesota
families to make music. Although he was born in Fargo and
later moved to Los Angeles after his first hit on Minnesota's
Soma Records to be closer to "the biz," one of Minnesota's
most highly decorated pop stars, Bobby Vee (nee Robert
Velline), moved back to Minnesota in 1981. He came with
his wife, three sons and daughter and now makes a home in
the St. Cloud area while still touring around the world and in
this country, often with other early rock 'n' roll hitmakers like
Little Eva, Brian Hyland, Lou Christie, Fabian and others.
Although often unfairly pigeonholed in the "teen idol" period
prior to the UK invasion and after the ascension of Elvis,
Vee's stats and impact are as impressive as any.

With 38 songs in the top 100 charts, six gold singles,
14 Top 40 hits and two gold albums (just in the United
States alone), *Billboard* called him "one of the top 10 most
consistent chartmakers ever." He was often on popular teen
TV shows in the '60s like *American Bandstand*, *Shindig* and
*Where the Action Is*, and made a handful of movies. In 1995
the British '60s music magazine *The Beat Goes On* fans voted
Vee the Best International Act and in 1994 and named him
runnerup to Sir Paul McCartney in the category of Most
Accomplished Performer. Still active in the studio and on the
road, today he is backed by The Vees (featuring his two sons
Jeff and Tommy, Jeff Olsen, George Mauer and the sizzling

Bobby Vee in 1959: The young rocker's bittersweet start in the music business before he became
tagged as a "Teen Idol" after moving to Los Angeles, is seen in action here before the time
of his Soma Records hit "Suzy Baby."
(photo: courtesy Bobby Vee and The Vees)

guitarist and bandleader Ar J. Stevens). Vee's other son, Robby, has an escalating solo career and occasionally works with the Vees, while his daughter Jennifer runs a respected design and graphics company.

Velline's break into the music came very early, but was bittersweet at best. He was just a sophomore in high school when he and his brother Bill's band, The Shadows, were called to play a Moorhead gig, after Buddy Holly's plane went down outside Clearlake, Iowa, Feb. 3, 1959, en route to the Minnesota date. Vee would later honor that dark start in music with a beautiful 40th anniversary Buddy Holly tribute album in 1999 called *Down the Line*. (He also cut a record with Holly's surviving band, The Crickets, in 1962.) For many years, every February, he's been a regular headliner at the annual Winterland Dance Party at Clearlake's Surf Ballroom, the site of Holly's last live show.

Still true to his rockabilly roots and with a great ear for timeless pop, in 2005 he released a smart, engaging collection of original songs on his own Rockhouse label with his family band and musical friends, *Last of the Great Rhythm Guitar Players*. In 2006, Vee and a few "teen idol" stars parked their acts in Branson for a live multimedia show that has been packing them in. Called "The Original Stars of American Bandstand," the rock 'n' roll show features Vee, Fabian, The Chiffons, Brian Hyland and Chris Montez and plays (where else?) Dick Clark's American Bandstand Theater. Besides having a spectacular run, Vee and company also have played at Sir Andrew Lloyd Webber's 50th birthday celebration, the world-renowned Sydmonton festival, and done gigs with

McCartney in both New York and London for McCartney's "Buddy Holly Festivals." If there were any justice in rock 'n' roll history, Bobby Vee would have been inducted into the Rock 'n' Roll Hall of Fame a long time ago.

Without question, The Peterson Family is *the* First Family of Minnesota Music. Their story is remarkable not only for their innumerable credits individually but how the Peterson name has become synonymous for expert musicianship and inspired artistry, from 85-year-old Jeanne Arland Peterson (the pianist, singer and mother who still performs) to her gifted children, Linda, Patty, Billy, Ricky and Paul.

You could never make up the Peterson family saga: It's like the *Sound of Music* crossed with *Full House*, set perennially on the bandstand and packing a mighty swank – and funky – soundtrack. Or as popular jazz saxophonist and LA radio host Dave Koz notes, "There is no family in the world quite like the Petersons. First of all, there's like 700 of 'em, and each one more talented than the next. Hipper than The Osmonds, more soulful than The Jacksons, they even give The Von Trapps a run for their money! Anchored by the ageless grace, talent and inspiration of matriarch Jeanne, there is nothing that this family of incredible artists can't do. You name it, a Peterson is there to do it ... and *nail it*! I feel blessed to have shared the stage with many a Peterson, and even more blessed to call this incredible family my friends."

Jeanne was widowed in 1969 when her husband, Willie, died. The two worked together at WCCO radio and TV and also played organ at the old Met Stadium for Twins games. The hard-working matriarch and Minnesota Music Hall of Famer raised five kids, feeding them a fortified diet of jazz and spooning in a dash of pop for good measure. Proof that it worked? Each celebrated musician has his or her own solo albums, scads of awards, in-depth web sites and celebrated together again on the family's 20th anniversary Christmas show in 2006.

Writing a few years ago in *The Los Angeles Times*, Don Heckman tried to sum up everything Peterson: "When Linda Peterson talks about getting together for a jam session, she isn't kidding. The Minneapolis-based jazz singer can assemble a world-class band just by making a few phone calls to family members, including brother Billy, bassist for the Steve Miller Band (and lauded as one of the finest players in the industry), brother Ricky, who plays keyboards with David Sanborn (and recently finished working with contemporary star John Mayer) or little brother Paul (who's served as) musical director for Donny Osmond." The music scribe goes on to enumerate her strengths as a "mature...splendid jazz performer...Like Carmen McRae, Peterson is a good enough pianist to supply substantial and fittingly intimate self-accompaniment."

Missing in this chummy overview, however, is Patty, seven-time winner of the Minnesota Music Award as Best Female Vocalist and Best Jazz Group, and possessed, *Downbeat* magazines sighs, of "forthright sexiness and spunk." You've probably heard her lovely and versatile voice on local and national commercial spots as well as hosting occasionally over WCCO-AM.

Her youngest brother, Paul, was prominent in the Prince camp, recording with and working in The Time, The Family and later as "St. Paul," before the multi-instrumentalist, record producer and songwriter went on to work with everyone from The Osmonds as the band leader on Donny and Marie's TV show to Jonny Lang, The Corrs, The Spice Girls, Neneh Cherry, Shannon Curfmann, Tuck & Patty, Anita Baker, Paula Abdul, Sergio Mendes, Oleta Adams and – like his siblings – many, many more. Don't worry about the lineage continuing. The grandchildren are stepping out more frequently with their elders in the Minnesota family jam session that never ends.

It's a long way from the South Pacific Island of Tonga to the land of the Petersons, the Johnsons and other good Scandinavians. Imagine the region's collective surprise when another family band, The Jets, sired by Maikeli "Mike" and Vaké Wolfgramm, surfaced, in the lutefisk center of North America. Eight of the kids (Leroy, Eddie, Eugene, Haini, Rudy, Kathi, Elizabeth and Moana Wolfgramm) played in the band. Nine more were at home!

Music industry veteran Don Powell, who had a hand in the careers of David Bowie, Stevie Wonder and others, discovered them one night at a suburban supper club in the early-'80s. They had gotten stranded in the area when the hotel they were playing another gig at went bankrupt. Powell took them under his wing, and later secured an MCA Records deal, which proved fruitful for everybody. The Polynesian pop and dance band produced eight top-10 hits, along with six albums, performed on

TV shows like *Webster*, *Oprah*, *Joan Rivers*, *Live with Regis*, *Arsenio Hall* and later BET.

The Jets even landed their own Disney Special, *The Jets In Hawaii*, the first Disney music special to air on the new Disney Channel in 1987.

Quickly acknowledged as part of the Minneapolis Sound, the heavily R&B-influenced band became so big in the late-'80s, that an upcoming group called New Kids on the Block opened for them on tour, according to The Jets' web site. They also played at the 1988 Seoul Summer Olympics and the 2002 Winter Olympics in Salt Lake City. Many of the original members eventually went off to less successful solo paths. The group today, still comprised of younger Wolfgramm members – and a next generation of Jets – plays more Christian-oriented music. But their chapter in Minnesota's music history is definitely a big family affair – with no end in sight. ♪

Bobby Vee with his sons, The Vees, who regularly back him at gigs all over the world.
(photo: courtesy of Bobby Vee and The Vees)

The Jets pictured here for their greatest hits album.
(photo: courtesy of The Jets)

Four of the Wolfgramms in a recent photo. The band reached the charts in the '80s with hits like
"You Got It All" and "Crush On You."
(photo: courtesy of The Jets)

The young Jeanne Arland Peterson.
(photo: courtesy of the Peterson family)

The Peterson Family (left to right: Patty, Linda, Jeanne, Billy, Paul, Ricky) with one of the
Grands (Jason, Linda's son), who often plays with the family.
(photo: courtesy of the Peterson family)

Dave Ray (1943-2002): A master bluesman, band leader, poet, record producer, ranter and a key part of the legendary folk-blues trio Koerner, Ray and Glover.
(photo: Greg Helgeson)

# The 1960s-'70s Minnesota Folk Scene
## *Changing Times in Minnesota Music*

S ay the word "coffeehouse" today and most people think of the big corporate coffee sellers, or their quaint little neighborhood coffee shop where the laptops hang out. But 30 to 40 years ago, coffeehouses fueled Minnesota's acoustic and folk music scene, giving rise to a host of internationally known players, indie record labels, radio shows and a rarified collection of colorful pickers, cowboy minstrel poets, buskers, bluesers, autoharpists and singer-songwriter types. Where now you can often buy hip recordings from coffee-shops like Starbucks and Caribou, yesteryear's destination java joints featured Minnesota's finest acoustic musicians making live music.

The Twin Cities folk scene of the early-'60s through the '70s produced some of the most culturally significant and enduring music made in Minnesota. Although it was never destined – or intended – to be as commercially successful as the rock, funk and pop records made here during different periods, its timeless appeal still holds sway. Back in the early days of Garrison Keillor's then little-known *A Prairie Home Companion* radio show, the scene regularly served as the show's magical musical pipeline. And even today, it continues to draw on acoustic acts and individuals like Adam Granger, Bob Douglas and Pop Wagner, the cowboy poet, rope tricker, fiddler and all-around folkie whose jokes are as sharp as his licks and lariat. Their musical depth and endearing stage performances are still giving the Old Scout (Keillor) and shy people everywhere the will "to get up and do what needs to be done."

By the start of this new century, the landmark coffeehouses in Stadium Village and Dinkytown that gave folkies a place to play had long disappeared. The Ten O'clock Scholar (eventually the site of a Burger King) in Dinkytown where a young Bob Dylan shared the stage with Spider John Koerner, burned down. The Purple Onion, The Coffee Break and The Broken Drum all eventually shuttered for one reason or another.

And that comfortable place upstairs? That second-floor folk emporium where celebrated songwriter Greg Brown debuted in Minneapolis, where Minneapolis' own Peter Lang played his six- and 12-string style of classic American guitar and the young songwriter Ann Reed honed her craft – the one with a couple big stuffed funky chairs and folding seats that for a long time anchored the West Bank acoustic scene and played host to talent from out of town, The Coffeehouse Extempore? The Extemp closed and faded into history in 1987, leaving behind indelible memories of great performances by guitar virtuosos such as Tim Sparks and Phil Heywood, fiddlin' Mary DuShane or Larry Long (whom Studs Terkel called "a true American troubadour"). Long's tales and songs from the road (often with his faithful dog, Dubious, whether about serenading the "tractorcade" in Washington, D.C., for a historic farmer's rally or his storied visits to the Rosebud Indian Reservation) continues today as he writes his own tunes and collaborative songs with kids and the elderly in different communities across the land.

Red Nelson, an intoxicating storyteller who owned the Scholar and threw legendary rent parties, and Maury Bernstein, a walking ethnomusicologist, folk music radio host and part-time musician, were as influential "folkers" as the folkies that they befriended, entertained and occasionally educated with their hospitality, chutzpah and scene-making.

The proximity of the University of Minnesota to the Extemp and other coffeehouses was critical to the acoustic music artists who set the folk scene on fire. It attracted talent from all over the place with cool, antiquated-sounding names like Papa John Kolstad, playing inscrutable repertoires that ran from Djanjo Reinhardt to obscure jug bands, labor movement songs and bluegrass masters. Dinkytown's busy street corners and the curbsides of the West Bank provided ample space for pickers and grinners like Jerry Rau, Gail Heil, Bob Bovee and others to play on when moved to play alfresco for spare change and the thrill of making music. Young students, some of whom would drop out to adopt the bohemian lifestyle spawned by the beatniks of the '50s and early-'60s, filled the ranks and became fans of the music. Even the school's deep faculty, including professors like Henry Blackburn and others, proved to be good practitioners of folk, blues and jazz music, with record collections that blew the mind and fed the soul.

The acoustic front would later form a launching pad, in part, for the whole counterculture era. That period produced its own musicians, record labels such as Train on the Island and Mill City Music, and an underground press like *One Hundred Flowers* and *The Little Sandy Review*, started by Jon Pankake and the late Paul Nelson, who later became one of *Rolling Stone's* most formidable music writers. It also provided the soundtrack for the lives of the growing number of political proponents for civil and student rights that were later followed by legions of anti-Vietnam war protesters.

"Spider" John Koerner came to the U from upstate New York, fell in with local players Dave "Snaker" Ray (also a university student) and self-made hipster and blues scholar Tony "Little Sun" Glover, and created Koerner, Ray and Glover, an acoustic trio that played country blues, traditional folk tunes and the occasional original, like Willie Murphy's and Koerner's "I Ain't Blue" (which later turned up on Bonnie Raitt's first album, produced by Ray at his homemade Minnesota studio).

The trio made a long string of records together and in various solo or one-two combinations over the years, among them the essential *Blues, Rags & Hollers* for Elektra (later re-released on the Twin Cities' Grammy Award-winning Red House Records, founded by Bob Feldman, who died tragically early in 2006). They played historic music festivals such as Newport in '65, and their records turned up in the personal collections of John Lennon, Beck, Mick Jagger, Jim Morrison, Eric Clapton and others.

Through the years, Glover, who penned best-selling books about how to play the harmonica, has sat in live with everyone from rockers like The Doors and David Johannsen (New York Dolls) to Patti Smith and others. In 1986, he made a compelling two-hour documentary about the trio, *Blues, Rags & Hollers: The Koerner, Ray & Glover Story*, and in 2005 was often a focal point in the Martin Scorsese 2005 documentary about Dylan, *No Direction Home*. Filmmaker

Don McGlynn produced a similar film about Spider John the same year.

"This is how it was," Glover told the monthly *Sweet Potato* music paper (which later became *City Pages*) in 1981: "I was Sonny Terry, Dave was Leadbelly and John was Woody Guthrie." In a period where nonconformists were abundant, KR&G out-nonconformed everyone. Many times onstage, their feet were tapping – but all in different time! Koerner, who is also an avid astronomer, often told long, screwy jokes wearing a head umbrella, while the trio's set list visited Lead Belly, Memphis Minnie, Muddy Waters, Sleepy John Estes, Robert Johnson, Peg Leg Howell and Bukka White, and others. Ray, who formed various electric and acoustic bands over time, from Bamboo and Snaker to The Waist Band and The Three Bedroom Ramblers, is remembered not only as a finely articulate bluesman, folkie and rocker but also as a first-class ranter, capable of teeing off on just about any subject. Later in his life Ray became a master of his work. He died of cancer on Thanksgiving 2002.

No look back the coffeehouse scene would be complete without some discussion of some the other artists and composers it has produced – Sean Blackburn and Dakota Dave Hull, Bill Hinkley and Judy Larson and Peter Ostroushko. Like many others touched on here, they each deserve their own chapter. In their day, Sean and Dave revitalized the Western Swing music of Moon Mullican, Bob Wills, Adolph Hofner and others. Their records together on Flying Fish, Biscuit City and Train on the Island are collector's items. Blackburn, who died in 2005, sang in a beautiful baritone in which he could also romantically yodel, while Hull has been called "one of the best guitarists in the world" by a fellow folkie from the Greenwich Village scene (and a former roommate of Dylan's when he first blew into to New York from Minneapolis), the late, always great Dave Van Ronk.

Hull plays and records frequently today with Kari Larsen. As noted on their web site, "Hull and Larson's musical mansion has many rooms, reflecting their encyclopedic knowledge – and command – of folk, pop, world, jazz, and classical musics. Here you'll find Appalachian tunes, ragtime, Irish airs, Western swing, Brazilian melodies, Tin Pan Alley, and original compositions drawing on these influences and more."

Hinkley and Larson, on the other hand, who met in the Sorry Muthas jug band in 1970, readily define and redefine the term "buskers."  And while there are many buskers in the world's subways, parks, taverns, clubs and wedding halls, there is probably no folk duo like them on the planet. Fine instrumentalists on mandolin, banjo, guitar and fiddle and powerfully personal singers with a droll sense of humor, their deep knowledge of music extends from the fiddle and guitar traditions of the British, Scottish and Irish to Scandinavia, South America and all parts USA. Hinkley was inducted into the Minnesota Music Hall of Fame in New Ulm, and both received a lifetime achievement award from the Minnesota Bluegrass and Oldtime Music Association in 2000. Just one listen to their masterpiece double album, *Out in Our Meadow*, will show why these two are treasures of the Minnesota folk world.

With his Ukrainian roots, great ear, fleet fingers and big heart, plus more than 1,000 credits on other musicians' albums and his own must-own CDs, Peter Ostroushko just might be the living embodiment of Minnesota's folk music era, now in its fifth or sixth decade. The master mandolinist and fiddler has played for theater, television and film productions and for a year led Keillor's house band, The Powdermilk Biscuit Band (aka The New Prairie Ramblers). Ostrousko can play in any style or setting, whether it's live or in studio with Emmylou Harris, Norman Blake, Taj Mahal or the Minnesota Symphony Orchestra. Proficient and profound, Ostroushko often can, as a composer and a sideman, blend genres in what he calls in his web biography *slüz düz* music, a phrase borrowed from his mother, meaning, roughly, "over the edge" or "off his rocker." It goes down great with a big pint, or a good cup of joe.

Today live music and coffeehouses are slowly coming full circle. St. Paul's Gingko's Coffeehouse has been featuring musicians for a decade or more, but increasing numbers of places in the suburbs, from the School of Wise out in Victoria to the 318 Wine and Coffee Bar in Excelsior (which occasionally hosts Michael Monroe and many other familiar names and new talents) are featuring live music again. But if you're simply nostalgic for the old West Bank scene, take in a show at the Cedar Cultural Center, the larger showcase venue for broadly defined folk music talent from across the globe. It's just down the block from the Extemp site, and still caters to the eclectic tastes and quality musicianship that has always been a hallmark of the area's folk music history. As they used to say, it will help you get your head together. ♪

Pop Wagner: Cowboy minstrel poet, lariat master, horseman and fiddler.
(photo: Greg Helgeson)

Spider John Koerner, Tony "Little Sun" and Dave "Snaker" Ray: An alternative photo taken for their legendary *Blues, Rags & Hollers* debut album that influenced everyone from John Lennon and Mick Jagger to The Doors, Beck and others.
(photo: courtesy The Paul Nelson Archives and Koerner, Ray and Glover)

Bill Hinkley and Judy Larson: Brilliant buskers with a world of folk music at their fingertips.
(photo: Greg Helgeson)

Larry Long, "A true American troubador," says Studs Terkel.
(photo: Greg Helgeson)

The Twin Cities' fertile folk music scene regularly contributed musicians to Garrison Keillor's renowned *Prairie Home Companion* radio show back during the '70s and continues to do so today. (photo: courtesy *Prairie Home Companion*, Dana Nye photographer)

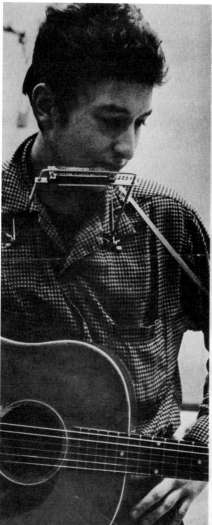

Handbill from one of Bob Dylan's first New York gigs in 1963.

# Bob Dylan
## *Bringing It All Back Home*

A rtists who define and transform culture through time and generations are rare. Think of William Shakespeare, Miguel Cervantes, Picasso, Beethoven or Louis Armstrong. Add native son Bob Dylan to the list. For more than 45 years Dylan's songwriting has embraced and merged such a wide range of styles and themes that his work will still be religiously pored over into the next century by fans, songwriters, academics, writers and any unfortunate musician who gets damned with the praise "the next Bob Dylan." Even his most flawed work — a handful of albums from different periods, but mostly his widely panned movies (*Renaldo and Clara*, 1975, and *Masked and Anonymous*, 2003) — get more scrutiny than one can imagine.

Unlike Americans, the Irish have never given up on their music roots, Dylan once noted to U2's Bono in a *Rolling Stone* interview. If nothing else, Dylan has been a soul keeper of America's musical traditions, its rhythm and blues, folk, gospel, country western and early rock 'n' roll, each genre with its own regal bloodlines. Dylan borrowed, bootlegged, mixed, honored and rewrote them all in a singular voice and a magical manner of phrasing that many have emulated, or mocked, but that few have ever mastered.

Through 44 studio and live albums between 1963 and today, his storied lyrics allude to everything from philosophy to surrealism, the Bible, Broadway, Bertolt Brecht, Tin

Pan Alley, baseball, Minnesota coordinates (Wabasha Street, Highway 61, et al) and the visionary high ground of America's beat poets like Lawrence Ferlinghetti and Allen Ginsberg. His many haunting songs about corrupted power, and the simple twists of fate that no one can control, often compassionately embrace or matter-of-factly describe the downtrodden, the man with the wrong colored skin, the murdered house maid felled by an upper class baron and the outcast. And of course the complexities of love and friendship, solitude and seeking, and the simple refuges of just living a life. As he proudly told this writer during a 1983 interview for *City Pages* with the release of his *Infidels* album, "No one has ever done what I've done before." Most likely no one will be able to do it again. Of his ragged singing style, even Bob admitted he's never been able to get used to the sound of his own voice: "It makes you want to hide."

Dylan remains one of America's most influential artists, and the world has recognized him as such with honorary degrees from universities and medals for artistic merit from the governments of France and the United States. He's been awarded two Grammys, a Golden Globe, an Academy Award and even a nomination for a Nobel Prize for Literature for *Chronicles, Volume I* (2004), his must-read, always-eloquent autobiography. Rich with poignant and often surprisingly candid looks into select times in his life, it includes tales of a middle class childhood in Hibbing and Duluth, where he was born in 1941.

Now at 65, when most his age are finished working, the blue-eyed native son is "still on the road, headed to another joint" as he sang in "Tangled Up in Blue" on his legendary *Blood on the Tracks* album, part of which he re-recorded with a slate of Twin Cities musicians at Sound 80 in 1974 with Bill Berg, Billy Peterson, Chris Weber, Peter Ostroushko, Kevin Odegard and Gregg Inhofer. His "Never Ending Tour" has literally been around the world several times, stopping at such disparate places such as Bologna, Budokan and Bismarck. Asked in '83 if he would ever retire, he scoffed at the idea. "Muddy Waters never retired. James Brown never retired. Why would I retire?!" His most recent work certainly affirms those sentiments. Released in late August 2006, Dylan's album *Modern Times* earned more critical raves and landed him his first No. 1 record since 1976's *Desire*.

Dylan's story and his enduring ties to Minnesota – then and now – are worth noting. At an early age up on the Range, the young Robert Allen Zimmerman did what most Midwestern kids would do at night when locked in remote towns in the '50s and '60s: Dial in the rock 'n' roll stations from distant places and escape into the spectral reaches of the atmosphere. One intergalactic outpost in Shreveport, La., Stan's Record Shop, beamed R&B, doo wop and Little Richard's seminal rock 'n' roll songs to strangers in different places who could pick up the signal and order records from what must have seemed like a life-saving playlist. Today Dylan's come full circle with his own radio show on the XM satellite called "Theme Time Radio Hour with Bob Dylan."

While in 1957 at Jewish summer camp called Herzl Camp just outside the Twin Cities, the teenager from Hibbing met another devotee of Stan's, a St. Paul kid named Larry Kegan. Kegan's own story is available online at larrykegan.com. The two became lifelong friends, cutting a 78 rpm record together as teenagers one afternoon for $5 at a simple recording studio with another pal. They did a medley of doo wop, R&B and Little Richard bits, and so for five bucks and a few laughs among friends, Bob Dylan's illustrious recording career was born on a quick-press record.

After high school, he briefly played keyboards and did handclaps in Bobby Vee's band using the pseudonym Elston Gunnn (sic). When he returned to the Twin Cities, entering the University of Minnesota for a short time only, the Hibbing hepcat who wrote in his high school yearbook that he was going off to join Little Richard's band, discovered that the coffeehouse scene around the campus didn't brook much rock 'n' roll. Folk music, played by college dropouts, fellow students, a few profs and some self-made ramblers at the height of the beatnik period, was the thing. Dylan momentarily abandoned his road to Little Richard and took up the soup du jour, playing with and learning from folkies like Spider John Koerner, Tony "Little Sun" Glover, Dave Ray and others. When he later left for New York, his bootcamp intro to folk music 101 in the University scene served him well.

In New York, Dylan would rewrite what was on the menu, change up all the canons, ballads and conceits and make rain of his new name that he first coined in Minneapolis.

In a Terry Gross interview on "Fresh Air" in 1999 with Bobby Vee to discuss Vee's 40th anniversary tribute album to Buddy Holly (*Down The Line*), Vee recalled how he was walking through Greenwich Village one day in the early-'60s and spied a poster for a Bob Dylan concert: He told Gross, laughing, "Gee, that looks a lot like Elston Gunnn!"

The acute details of Dylan's journey of self-discovery in New York are beautifully recollected in *Chronicles*. So is the bitterness on the other side of the coin called fame. He consistently shunned the laudatory titles thrown at him as "spokesman for a generation" and other press hype, as we learn in his book and the award-winning 2005 Martin Scorsese documentary for PBS, *No Direction Home*. Wanting only to freely lead his life, write songs and raise a family out of the public eye, the once self-described "song-and-dance man" has retained some level of valued anonymity while personally – if maybe not intentionally – contributing to "the myth of Bob Dylan" in rarely given interviews and explanations about his work and who he is.

Strolling one time with a friend past a window where a cool set of clothes was on display, he reportedly remarked, "Now that's something Bob Dylan would wear." That off-the-cuff comment says more about how Dylan views himself at one deep level than all of the tomes written about him. If he ultimately can't be known solely through his words and music, other artists have stepped forward recently to probe and celebrate the artist and the enigma, including choreographer Twyla Tharp, whose musical *The Times They Are A-Changin'* strung together 90-minutes of Dylan tunes (and bombed on Broadway). In 2007, look for a movie about him, starring a host of actors playing the main man, plus actress Cate Blanchette.

These days, Dylan still visits Minnesota, where he keeps a home, plus he occasionally pulls into town on the Never Ending Tour. His roots run as long and winding as the Mississippi River, but his artistry knows no bounds. Perhaps that's why so many worldwide have looked to his songs to find some direction home. "People want to know where I'm at 'cuz they don't know where they're at," he snapped in 1983. Most likely, not much has changed since then. The rock 'n' roll bard of the north country fair has triumphantly ridden bareback through the territory, leaving the mapmaking to us. ♪

The mythology about Bob Dylan almost equals the weight of his inspired music through the years.
(photo: Associated Press)

One of the world's most famous and influential artists has preserved America's rich musical culture while rewriting much of it in his own hand.
(photo: courtesy Columbia Records)

Queen of folk, Joan Baez, joins the blue-eyed native son around the time of Dylan's
Rolling Thunder Revue band.
(photo: Associated Press)

"Bob Dylan: The 30th Anniversary Concert Celebration" in rehearsal at Madison Square Garden,
October 16, 1992. Shown from left: Roger McGuinn, G.E. Smith, Ron Wood, George Harrison,
Bob Dylan, Duck Dunn, Tom Petty, Neil Young and Steve Cropper.
(photo: courtesy Columbia Records)

# Minnesota Rhythm and Blues Giants

D r. John stood watching the master on the piano. He shook his head. The wrong cat is headlinin' tonight, he growled to no one in particular in his signature New Orleans drawl, leaning against the wall near the dressing room just off the stage. Onstage at First Avenue, Minneapolis' Midnight Mayor, the former patron saint of the West Bank and the legendary leader of Willie and the Bees, Willie Murphy, was driving through an array of R&B, jazz, boogie woogie and original numbers that were out- trickin' the famous Mac Rebennack, more commonly known as Dr. John.

Mistaken roles and missed chances have occasionally spiked the life and times of Willie Murphy. But the truth be told, there's only one other *badder* musician in both towns, and he quickly moved to live first in a purple house in suburbia a long time ago. It's been true for countless years that the multi-instrumentalist, soul singer, songwriter, record producer and rabid film aficionado many have mistaken for a black man is really a lived-in Irish Catholic. Just ask Maurice Jacox, Murphy's former Bumblebees' sax player who *is* African-American, the guy who had to set the record straight for the 14 years that the Bees made honey. Covering and writing funk jams, R&B obscurities and roof-raising rock 'n' roll on record and onstage with a power and passion not seen since with players like John Beach on keyboards (who was almost as renowned as the groovy King Bee), that band in the '70s just simply tore it up anytime they buzzed the hive.

Murphy doesn't just loom large in Minnesota's music; he's front and center and much appreciated in Europe. Accord-

Willie & The Bees (Murphy, right, in shades): One of the pillars of the Minnesota music story whose legendary R&B sound helped put the West Bank music scene on the map.
(photo: Greg Helgeson)

ing to the Blues on Stage web site, he "was named one of the three charter members of the Minnesota Music Hall of Fame, along with Bob Dylan and Prince. Over the years, the nationally known and respected Minnesota Music Association has given more nominations and awards to Willie and his groups than anyone else." Anyone who saw them at their peak in West Bank joints like The Triangle Bar or Dania Hall, or who caught Murphy playing his long-running solo gig at the Viking until the bar was suddenly closed in August 2006 after 47 years, knows that the Bees are one of the pillars of the Minnesota music story.

In his time, Murphy turned down a job at Elektra Records in the early-'70s as a producer, when hippie (i.e. anti-establishment) ethics prevailed, because he didn't want to move to either coast, or be perceived as "selling out." That decision was a blessing for this community at large and his own charged musical output since, including brilliant solo work like his album *Willie Murphy Hits Piano/Piano Hits Willie Murphy* on his own label, Atomic Theory Records, and with his current band, Angel-Headed Hipsters. Like many of America's R&B heavyweights, he is admired as much abroad as he is in his own hometown.

For a time, the original Willie in the Bees was Willie Walker, initially a gospel singer from the South who was well-suited to The Bees' soul attack. Walker cut some sides for the Memphis-based Goldwax Records in the '60s and was once offered the opportunity to join the legendary Curtis Mayfield. Perhaps the most invisible of all the R&B legends in Minnesota, Walker is also among the genre's most impressive stylists, plus an early influence on a bunch of south Minneapolis teenagers who caught his act at the Nacirema Club, among them Jimmy Jam and Prince. Appearing regularly now with The Butanes, who have backed conceivably every important blues and soul singer of the past 20 years, Walker is enjoying something of a renaissance and a much higher profile the past few years. He recorded three widely acclaimed CDs, one self-titled, the other two with The Butanes called *Right Where I Belong* and *Memphisapolis*. The last one was issued in October 2006, and all are getting worldwide attention.

Both Willies and other keepers of the R&B tradition in the Twin Cities share historical bonds, as well as quite a few notes, with their predecessors such as Leonard "Baby Doo" Caston, Lazy Bill Lucas, Cornbread Harris and Auburn Pat Hare. Caston (1917-1987) worked with The Big Three Trio during the '40s with Willie Dixon and Ollie Crawford, eventually settling in north Minneapolis and playing clubs and recording a bit, after a stretch in the Chicago blues scene after the war.

Lazy Bill Lucas still has a KFAI radio show named in his honor, which was picked up by the late Joel Johnson (also an admired blues player and lover). Lazy Bill mentored the Bees, blues harp player Lynwood Slim, Lamont Cranston and others. He died in 1982 at age 64. Blistering blues guitarist Pat Hare recorded and worked with James Cotton and the mighty Muddy Waters. But when he moved to Minneapolis in the '60s and played with then-resident bluesman Mojo Buford and others, his life spun out of control one night in a domestic dispute. He was later convicted of murder. Hare went to Stillwater prison, where he died in 1980, just about a month before his life sentence was to be commuted.

James Samuel "Cornbread" Harris, one of the area's remaining senior blues and jazz players as he nears 80, can still be found in the clubs. He's also the father of super-Flyte Tyme producer and songwriter, Jimmy Jam Harris. One of his early career highlights was his collaboration with Augie Garcia in 1955 to record "Hi Ho Silver," according to Cornbread's web site. But five decades later, Harris' vigor and vast repertoire can still charm the casual nightcubber, or the ardent hipster.

Although he's not pushing the octogenarian envelope yet, Pat Hayes has had his mojo working with the Lamont Cranston Band almost as long as the various blues legends he's been influenced by, from Albert King on guitar to Little Walter on blues harp. The Hamel, Minn., native formed the Cranstons (named after the '40s radio figure of the same name whose trademark line was "The Shadow knows") with his guitarist brother, Larry, after first trying his hand as a folkie on the West Bank.

Larry Hayes' swinging original tune, "Excusez Moi Mon Cheri," was cut by The Blues Brothers (Dan Aykroyd and John Belushi) on the flipside hit of their remake of the old Sam & Dave classic "Soul Man." Larry's been out of the Cranston picture for years, and Aykroyd has become a long-time friend to Pat and his band, as has Bonnie Raitt, with whom one incarnation of the band toured through the Colorado Rockies in 1980.

Working with well-known players such as ace songwriter and keyboard player Bruce McCabe, the Bingham Brothers Charlie and Bob, and others, the band hitched its blooze wagon to Rolling Stones tour in 1981, opening three Midwest dates with the launch of one of their collectible Waterhouse Record albums, *Shakedown*. McCabe, who would one day cut his own fine solo records, later teamed up with Charlie Bingham to form the Bingham-McCabe Band and later the popular Hoopsnakes before taking a seat in the Jonny Lang group.

Twenty-five years after the tour, you can still see why Hayes and his players have had such a long run on concert and barroom stages big and small, give or take gaps where they broke up, then reunited to play the blues, swing tunes and shuffles. Just one listen to their own "E Jam" (penned in the smoky haze when gigging) and attendance at joints like St. Paul's dark River Serpent on the banks of the Mississippi, or along the urban railroad tracks at The Cabooze (a coming of age ritual required for any music lover) – and you'll understand why real epiphanies happen at Lamont Cranston gigs on any given night.

Of all the blues-driven singers in bands – from the Minnesota Barking Ducks and Inside Straight to the soulful Explodo Boys, Mick Sterling's Stud Brothers, Curt Obeda's Butanes, and legions of lesser-knowns – none could sing or mesmerize like Doug Maynard. Maynard, plus a string of talented roadhouse bluesmen that also included Milwaukee Slim (the singing bus driver!), Big Walter Smith, Percy Strother, Sonny Rogers, Jim Miller, Roy Alstad, RJ Mischo, Teddy Morgan and others, kept alive the blues scene at clubs like Wilebski's in St. Paul's Frogtown, regardless of the size of their fan base. Maynard fronted several groups in the '70s, including Live Bait, Passage and Troubled Sleep (often with some of the best known "sidemen" in the region, Bobby "Kinky" Schnitzer and Bruce "Creeper" Kurnow). The atomic blues belter could break a note into two and three parts simultaneously so that it sounded like he was harmonizing with himself. And he could sing with so much raw emotion and the command of the most gifted gospel and soul singers that he would regularly pack clubs like the Union Bar, Moby Dicks and other joints whenever he played.

Somewhere he picked up the nickname "The Dog" while voters in music polls and scribes such as Jon Bream at the *Star Tribune* consistently named him the best singer in the Twin Cities. Writing in the liner notes for *The Lullaby*, Maynard's 1981 Shadow Records album, Tony Glover called him "the man with the tri-tone" – and gave him a new handle, "The Voice." Maynard teamed up with two superb singers in their own right, Margaret Cox and Melanie Rosales, in 1980 to form The Doug Maynard Band, and backed Bonnie Raitt on a national tour in 1982.

But the son of a Pentecostal preacher struggled with drugs and alcoholism. In and out of treatment through the years, Maynard sang briefly with The Bingham-McCabe Band. But his sobriety always hung by a thread. His singular, primal vocal prowess is featured on the soundtracks of *Patti Rocks*, *The Personals* and *To Live and Die in LA*. Maynard lived, loved and, in 1991, died hard in the Twin Cities. He was only 40 years old. A 10-song tribute record on Cold Wind Records of all Maynard originals, sung by The Voice and backed by the many musicians who played with him through the years, later came out in his honor. Like an engraving on his tombstone, it was called *Lost in the Blues*. ♪

Lamont Cranston, with cofounder, guitarist, singer and harp Pat Hayes: Their fans include Bonnie Raitt (pictured here with band), The Blues Brothers and thousands of blues-rock fans everywhere. (photo: Greg Helgeson)

Doug Maynard: "The Voice" often cited as the best vocalist in the Twin Cities
until his tragic death at 40 in 1991.
(photo: Greg Helgeson)

Willie Walker (left), the original Willie in the Bees, and bandleader Curt Obeda of The Butanes: Happily making music together in Memphisapolis after Walker's long absence from the music scene. (photo: Doug Knutson)

The legendary blues giant, Willie Dixon (left), reunites with an old band member from the '40s, Baby Doo Caston. The two played together in the Big Three Trio during WWII. (photo: Greg Helgeson)

# Funkytown
## The Minneapolis Sound at the End of the Disco Era

*Born and raised in the Eastern Europe, behind the Iron Curtain, in 1980 I was 17. The one and only TV station had a 2 (two) hours a day broadcast, paying tribute to our dictator. The foreign music was forbidden. The only way to listen to music was during the night, on the radio, being careful not to be heard by the neighbors. The secret police was everywhere. Although strongly jammed, the Voice of America and the Free Europe radio stations (both on short waves) were our small windows to the free world.*

*Funkytown made me cry. For me, Funkytown was the supreme expression of the freedom that we didn't have at the time. I had no tape or cassette recorder, so I've recorded the song on my BRAIN. Among the whistles of the jamming stations, the song shined like a diamond in the mud. It was mine for ever. They could not take control over my brain…*

—Norin, writing on the Funkytown web site

Every summer produces "the big hit." In 1980 that hit was "Funkytown," an innovative assembly of pop styles honed in South Minneapolis that grooved from the strobe-lit rooms of American discos to the top of international record charts. You wouldn't expect one song to deserve a whole chapter in a book about Minnesota music. Not with the likes of Prince, Dylan and many others who have written far greater tunes and whose songwriting artistry is beyond comparison. But the truth is, you could write a whole book about "Funkytown"!

Steven Greenberg, 25 years after the Minnesota musician put "Funkytown" into the global consciousness with the biggest hit ever from Mid-America.
(photo: Tony Nelson)

Penned by Steven Greenberg under the band nom de plume Lipps Inc., "Funkytown" is the Minnesota music scene's great sonic centerpiece that reveals, in part, the state's spirited rock 'n' roll past while hinting at its hallowed future into the '80s and '90s. The little pied-piper keyboard hook that flows through the tune echoes the classic garage-band sound of Minnesota's '60s. And its R&B guitar vamp and sax break capture the popular bar band sounds of the earlier '70s. But "Funkytown's" pure dance-floor feeling underscores the last stages of the disco era fever as a new decade began in 1980. The No. 1 single ruled, while the obituaries for disco were being written; Lipps Inc. just put the funeral on hold.

If you're a culture junkie with a scorecard, you already know that this irresistible pop song is also one of the most licensed and heard songs in American popular music. At the end of 2005, "Funkytown" had sold an estimated 10 million copies in over 70 countries around the globe since its release 26 years ago in 1980. It has appeared in more than 30 international movies including *Shrek 2*, *Contact*, Mel Brooks' *History of the World* and others. It has aired in more than 30 TV shows such as *Will and Grace*, *The Simpsons*, *South Park*, *American Idol*, *Oprah*, *ER* and *Friends*, and driven big brand commercials for Nissan, FedEx, France's Areva Energy (where it is even the "hold" music for people calling its corporate offices), and others including Ore-Ida Funky Fries.

Major sporting events and public occasions – from the last Olympics in Italy to NBA basketball courts and major league baseball ballparks everywhere (The Yankees

included it on their team CD) – have used it to rally the
fans and lift spirits. And there are countless cover versions
of it from groups like U2 to Pseudo Echo, an Aussie band
that sent it up the rock charts again with a remake in 1987.
Drag Queen Ru Paul and punk poet Henry Rollins have also
worked the F-song, not to mention that it's been morphed
into bluegrass, Tex Mex and marching band arrangements.
It's also landed on three major video releases: *Beatmania*,
*March Madness 2006*, *Shrek 2* and *Dance Revolution Seven*.
Who would have guessed that one song could capture the
imagination of so many people worldwide?

Its story begins, however, in a simple Lake Calhoun
apartment, where the 28-year-old Greenberg was just fooling
around on his guitar when he struck the power riff that gave
him one of many hooks for the song. He had already tasted
some success with "Rock It," which climbed the Billboard
charts on an indie label Greenberg named Flight Records.
Besides creating the first portable dance station he dubbed
the "Discomobile," he also had produced Minneapolis
hard rock groups like Fairchild, Cain and Dame. They,
too, recorded for Flight Records, which he co-owned with
Reid McLean (who later booked pop music at Minnesota's
Orchestra Hall) and Marsh Edelstein (one of the most
exuberant managers and booking agents that ever worked in
the Minnesota music biz).

Recorded at the state-of-the-art Sound 80 just a few
blocks north off East Lake Street with David Z (nee Rivkin)
engineering (who later went on to work with Prince, Jonny
Lang, Fine Young Cannibals and others), "Funkytown"

emerged from the same legendary studio where Dylan had re-cut much of his five-star *Blood on the Tracks* album six years earlier in 1974 with Minnesota musicians Bill Berg, Billy Peterson, Chris Weber, Peter Ostroushko, Kevin Odegard and Gregg Inhofer. Greenberg embraced the punk ethos of the period, the do-it-yourself recording approach, playing and producing all the instruments except for a real string section, sax and Tom Riopelle's (Fairchild) guitar.

He wisely brought a former Miss Black Minnesota, Cynthia Johnson, in to sing the lead after considering other local singers such as Patty Peterson and the young Sue Ann Carwell, who would soon cut a couple records for Warner Brothers. A young 17-year-old kid named Prince Rogers Nelson across town was doing the same thing—writing, playing all the instruments and recording his own work. But it was Greenberg who would beat Prince to the charts and score the biggest hit ever from Minnesota, racing past The Castaways' "Liar Liar" from 1965, which climbed to No. 12, and The Trashmen's "Surfin' Bird," which flew to No. 4 late in 1963.

After being rejected by every major label, eventually Casablanca Records (a division of Polygram Records and now part of Universal Music Group) picked up "Rock It" and the other tunes Greenberg had penned for a debut album called *Mouth to Mouth*. Among them was "Funkytown." After being successfully tested in gay dance clubs and disco record pools for DJs here and around the country, it was released in January 1980. But by midsummer it was a monster smash on everyone's radio – except in its own backyard. Local program directors deemed it "too black."

With "Funkytown," The Minneapolis Sound was born, an informed but unassuming mixture of funk, rock, pop and high production values. It was seared onto the world map ultimately by the Prince camp a few years later. But its ironic pathfinder and the Godfather of The Minneapolis Sound – a bespectacled St. Paul Jewish kid, caught between the hard rock world of the local club scene and the gay disco underground – suddenly become one of the darlings of Casablanca Records and an overnight celebrity who appeared in magazines like *People* and *Rolling Stone* and who traveled well beyond the velvet rope at the legendary Studio 54 in New York.

For a very brief tour that included Duffy's, First Avenue, Mexico City and a few other stops, Greenberg put together a live Lipps Inc. band with Terry Grant on bass, Ivan Rafowitz and Peter Johnson on keyboards, Bobby Vandell on drums, Johnson on vocals and Bobby Schnitzer on guitar. Lipps went on to record three more records, "Pucker Up," "Designer Music" and "Four," and Greenberg eventually produced albums by The Suburbs, Sussman Lawrence and others.

But the legacy of "Funkytown" inspired other music-related endeavors: In 1995, Greenberg decided to give something back to the local music community by following five bands over the course of a three-year period in a movie about trying to make it, trying to scratch out their own "Funkytown," not unlike Michael Apted's movies about four people in England growing up over 25 years called *25 Up*. He followed Tina & The B-Sides, The Delilahs, Greazy

Meal, Iya (the white Rasta reggae songwriter and band leader) and The Found. Each has their own particular trials, character and sound, and *Funkytown: The Movie* unobtrusively captures the energy, ironies, little victories and sorrows of each story.

In the course of the film, however, Iya is murdered; The Delilahs break up on the day they are set to sign a lucrative national recording contract; throat surgery threatens to bring down Tina; and a key member of Greazy Meal is asked by friends and fellow players to leave. The movie set the stage for a similar TV show on VH1 a year later and predated the whole reality TV vibe by several years. This indie doc premiered in June 2000 online at www.mediatrip. com and appeared at several festivals. But critics savaged it at home.

For a time, using royalties that continue to pour in even to this date, Greenberg ran October Records and Funkytown Studios, recording albums by Willie Wisely, David Wolfenson, The Delilahs and The Honeydogs. Both endeavors proved to be a solid training ground for his gifted musician-producer nephew from Boston, John Strawberry Fields, who later went on in Los Angeles to produce such contemporary acts as Switchfoot, Mandy Moore, Clay Aiken and more. Royalties also helped fund a successful Internet design company in the early '90s called Designstein, which today still serves many major consumer brands in the marketplace.

For all its irresistible simplicity, "Funkytown" has left an indelible stamp on the culture. It was part of the Rock 'n' Roll Hall Fame's "One Hit Wonder" exhibit in

1995, and kids of all ages still sing along to it today at the Minnesota History Museum in a mock recording studio as part of the Minnesota music scene exhibit called "Sounds Good To Me." Maybe it's all those hooks and that disco beat. Or that it's really a place that is everywhere – and nowhere. But the song's universal message in its longing lyric still promises escape to "a place that's right for me" – a chance to get out, bust loose and get down for anyone hearing its siren call. Today it has its own website (www. funkytown.com), where "Funkytown" fans from all over the world share their stories and learn more about their favorite song. In 2006 – 26 years after its release, it still remains the biggest-selling single in PolyGram's history and a beacon in the history of Minnesota music. ♪

FOR WEEK ENDING MARCH 15, 1980

# 1 Single This Week
## FUNKYTOWN/
## ALL NIGHT DANCING
### Lipps, Inc.
(LP/12-inch*) NBLP7197

## Billboard
# DISCO TOP 60

STAR Performer — registering greatest proportionate upward progress this week

| THIS WEEK | LAST WEEK | TITLE-Artist-Label | | THIS WEEK | LAST WEEK | TITLE-Artist-Label |
|---|---|---|---|---|---|---|
| ☆ | 1 | FUNKYTOWN/ALL NIGHT DANCING—Lipps, Inc. Casablanca (LP/12-inch*) NBLP-7197 | | ☆ | 35 | I ZIMBRA—Talking Heads Sire (LP/12-inch*) SRK-6076 |
| ☆ | 3 | HIGH ON YOUR LOVE/HOT HOT (Give It All You Got)— Debbie Jacobs MCA (LP/12-inch*) MCA-3203 | | ☆ | 36 | TONIGHT'S THE NIGHT—Sharon Page Source/MCA (12-inch) SOR-13952 |
| 3 | 2 | AND THE BEAT GOES ON/CAN YOU DO THE BOOGIE/THE BOX—The Whispers Solar (LP/12-inch) BXL1-3521 | | 33 | 21 | DO YOU LOVE WHAT YOU FEEL/ANY LOVE—Rufus and Chaka MCA (LP/12-inch) MCA-5103 |
| 4 | 4 | EVITA—all cuts—Festival RSO (LP) RS-1-3061 | | ☆ | 42 | WE GOT THE FUNK—The Positive Force Turbo (12-inch) T-402 |
| 5 | 5 | VERTIGO/RELIGHT MY FIRE/FREE RIDE—Dan Hartman Blue Sky (LP/12-inch) LP-36302 | | 35 | 27 | THE VISITORS (remix)—Gino Soccio Warner/RFC (12-inch) DRCS-8904 |
| | | | | ☆ | NEW ENTRY | DO YOU WANNA BOOGIE, HUNH/I GOT THE FEELING/ONE-SIDED LOVE AFFAIR—Two Tons O' Fun |

Billboard Chart

David Z. and Steven Greenberg in the famous Sound 80 recording studio where Dylan re-cut
much of *Blood on the Tracks* in the mid-'70s.
(photo: Greg Helgeson)

Greenberg in 1980, with Cynthia Johnson, whose vocal on the big hit
helped drive it to the top of the pop charts everywhere.
(photo: Robert Whitman)

This 2005 Nissan print ad is just one of many high-end international marketing campaigns that
effectively utilized the "Funkytown" song and sensibility over the years.

Iya: The white Rasta, who died during the filming of *Funkytown: The Movie* also recorded for
October Records, another legacy of the "Funkytown" hit.
(photo: Greg Helgeson)

The Delilahs also recorded for October Records, and in the *Funkytown* movie, split up the day they were to sign a major record contract.
(photo: Greg Helgeson)

Tom Riopelle, guitarist and songwriter from the band Fairchild (see chapter 9) contributed to the recording of "Funkytown."
(photo: courtesy of Fairchild)

# Minnesota's New Wave Scene
## 1970s –'90s: The Twin/Tone Records Era

H ow else could you explain it, that time between 1976 and 1984, other than to throw some kind of quasi-cosmological South Minneapolis spin on it? Something like: The bars were aligned with the record store and label, the rock rags, studios and impresarios, the film crew and hangers on, all reeling under the shakin' firmament in the House of Rock.

It was the best of times. It was the best of times.

Not since the Soma Records era of the early-'60s would Minnesota (and the rock world in general) see another hyper-creative period like the one that exploded in the late-'70s and early-'80s. The local scene played out against the larger forces of a highly stagnant music industry. FM radio everywhere was being wickedly choked by the album-oriented rock (AOR) formula, the vestiges of more open programming long gone and in its place, the prog rock and arena rock of Kansas, Boston and Styx, et al. Disco, the once-underground domain of gay dance clubs, had been sucked decisively into the mainstream.

Like other burgeoning scenes around the country at the time, the Twin Cities punk and new wave movement went back to and forward with the basics and re-invented rock 'n' roll for the next 20 years or so. It happened so often, with so many bands and on so many nights — but only within a relatively limited geographical area. Clubs like Jay's Longhorn (first run by Jay Berine) and Sam's (now First Avenue and the

Chris Osgood, former leader of the 1970s Suicide Commandos punk power trio, strikes a Marlon Brando pose for posterity.
(photo: Greg Helgeson)

7th Street Entry) in downtown Minneapolis and later Duffy's, on 26th and 26th, just off East Lake Street, were the primary venues before the sound(s) became trendy and financially viable for other bars.

The Suicide Commandos (Chris Osgood, Steve Almaas and Dave Ahl) led the charge as early as autumn 1975. They set the frenetic pace and in many ways underscored an entire era with their lyrics from "Complicated Fun":

"The new wave is the old wave/'Cuz we know it all by heart/We're looking for an anthem/That we haven't torn apart...We gotta have fun..."

Like their New York-based punk rock peers The Ramones, the Commandos played short, loud, exhilarating original songs and cherry-picked covers for their live sets and records. The ever-affable Osgood is often cited as one of the three or four graces that were key in the Twin Cities' new wave uprising. Its mecca was Oar Folkjokeopus, a delightfully shabby, specialty record store at 26th and Lyndale Avenue in South Minneapolis owned by Vern Sanden, whose tastes in rockabilly were almost insatiable. Across the street from the store was a convenient bar with a holy jukebox called the CC Club, where many a thirst was drenched.

"Oarfolk," as it became widely known, had clerking behind its counter Seth "Andy" Schwartz, a journalist and musical brain trust from New York who wrote for *The Minnesota Daily* and later *Metropolis* (the city's earliest weekly along with *The Twin Cities Reader*) and homey Peter Jesperson, perhaps the greatest music fan ever born and a confessed British rock freak. Taking a cue from the gay clubs in town like Suttons and The

Saloon, both spun records at The Longhorn, a first for local rock clubs. Writing on Twin/Tone's web site, Jesperson called the record store haunt, "a clubhouse for musical misfits of all kinds. The ad in the yellow pages read Rock 'N' Roll Headquarters For The Midwest, and that was no exaggeration."

Even when Schwartz moved back East to start the influential *New York Rocker* 'zine (moving to Epic Records when that caper ended), he kept readers everywhere tuned in to Minneapolis-St. Paul bands like the dark and short-lived NNB, The Hypstrz, with brothers Bill and Ernie Batson, Run Westy Run, rockabilly band Safety Last and many others. In an era of re-invented pop and rock, sonic explorer-guitarist Steve Tibbetts thrived even further underground than his peers, often with local percussionist Marc Anderson, assorted vocalists and others. Tibbetts and company created dense and lithe atmospheric pieces that relied on distortion, ambient production layering, improvisation and fusions of all sorts, all imbued with an inspiring and evolving spirituality that later embraced the music of Tibet and the chants of Buddhist nuns. To date, he's made 11 albums, many for the international label ECM Records.

Like Soma Records before them, the Twin/Tone label responded to the recording and distribution needs and the preponderance of talent of the times. Along with entrepreneur and engineer/producer Paul Stark (who looked uncannily like Buddy Holly) and Charley Hallman (a sports writer for the *Pioneer Press* and another avid rock fan), all threw in enthusiasm, naiveté, financing and time to create Twin/Tone Records in 1977.

"There were so many great bands in Minneapolis in 1976-'77 that the scene sort of *forced* Twin/Tone into existence," says Jesperson today, now senior vice president/A&R for New West Records in Los Angeles. He went on to produce and promote more than 50 Twin/Tone bands, plus those he later worked with at an offshoot label called Medium Cool Records, among them four of Twin/Tone's biggest finds: Curtiss A, The Replacements, The Suburbs and Soul Asylum.

Commenting on other regional scenes with the same energy and indie entrepreneurship, he notes, "We were inspired by labels like Stiff (in the UK) and Beserkley (in the Bay area)." Locally, the rock floodgates were open and quickly catching up with a growing fan base. The long-running music publication, originally for musicians, *Connie's Insider* (published by the late Connie Hechter) was waning, and *Sweet Potato*, a new monthly music newspaper, was just starting in August of 1979. Its location just four blocks south of Oarfolk was telling. Over the years, the paper regularly provided needed exposure for new bands such as Figures, Fingerprints, The Magnolias and the tough-as-spikes Pistons, plus emerging studios like Blackberry Way and other indie labels. It also established the Minnesota Music Awards (in the tradition of the Connie Awards at the *Insider*). Eventually *Sweet Potato* evolved into *City Pages*.

Acknowledging where the label's roots lay and the principals' loyalties belonged, Twin/Tone produced two major album sampler packages called *Big Hits of Mid-America, Volumes III*, a double-disc set ('79) and *IV* ('86), a single album. During its history its catalog grew to more than 300 record releases, according to Twin/Tone's web site. Among that stash is a rare (now out-of-print) 12-inch picture disc by then-All Star Wrestler and future Minnesota Gov. Jesse "The Body" Ventura. The label moved into Cookhouse Studios on Nicollet Avenue South and changed the name to Nicollet Studio. It was the same location as the home of Kay Bank Studios and Soma Records in the '60s, and now the vinyl grooves of Minnesota's mightiest rock eras shared even more history.

When the sun went down, the sound duly rose. Even now, it seems hard to believe how many giants locally and internationally played the new wave clubs for very little dough in that period, including The Wallets (which Twin/Tone eventually signed). The Wallets were an incomparable band in a period showered with similar superlatives. Part performance art, part rock combo (complete with accordion), they were led by a musical mad hatter, former James Chance and the Contortionist's sideman and little genius, Steve Kramer. (Try to find the band's inspired "The Night Before Christmas" 45, or its simply wonderful *Catch a Falling Star* EP on Spiffola.) The Police (Sting's band), Talking Heads, Elvis Costello and the Attractions, the B52s and David Johansen's group (the former New York Dolls leader and legend), in one of the all-time greatest Minnesota rock shows ever at the club, all played the Longhorn.

Duffy's, under the then husband-and-wife team of Dan Johnson and Leslie Simon, did a remarkable job of showcasing a crashing eclectic mix well beyond the rock frontier. They booked the criminally under-appreciated Shangoya and later Ipso Facto, two of Minnesota's first reggae (and calypso) bands, Britain's two-tone ska-rock acts like The Specials and cosmic jazz marvel Sun Ra and His Arkestra and even Beat novelist William Burroughs!

First Avenue already had a previous reputation for live music in another era when it was known as The Depot. It's captured on film during a stopover with Joe Cocker's big 10-piece group live in 1970 in what remains one of the finer rock 'n'roll performance films *Mad Dogs and Englishmen*. Ten years later, between the club's Main Room and its matchbox space, Seventh Street Entry, the bands just kept on coming, with club manager Steve McClellan always scurrying through the joints wearing a bemused or crazed look – or both – for the entire period.

"Chainsaw," as rock writer P.D. Larson fondly dubbed him, had a lot to handle, whether playing host to surprise Prince and The Time gigs (see the next music book in the Minnesota Series), or making room for Africa's King Sunny Ade and his 22-piece African Beats. Meanwhile, he and staff also were busy slotting groups into the Entry that held forth usually to breathing-room only capacity, like the sweetly melodic but intense rockers The Phones (also on Twin/Tone); Trip Shakespeare (which would yield the creative forces for Semisonic, Dan Wilson and John Munson) blasting out their crowd singalong, "Tool Master of Brainerd"; or the aptly named noisefunkrockers Things that Fall Down.

There was even a highly influential all-girl group – an anomaly even for that progressive period – called Tetes Noires. They recorded three albums on two different labels, built a respectable following and paved the way later for groups such as the brash, distaff punk trio, Babes in Toyland and the less blunt threesome, ZuZu's Petals (another Twin/Tone act, featuring Laurie Lindeen, the future bride of Paul Westerberg, whose own rockscapades are chronicled in her 2007 memoir *Petal Pusher*).

But the climaxes and antics weren't limited to just the bars, nor were they just grounds for fodder for the print media. Many were being preserved on film and video. Before there were MTV rock vids, rock video pioneer Chuck Statler and his trusty four-man Location Services crew had made raucous and funny films and video clips for bands like his former college pals Devo in Akron, Ohio, then Elvis Costello, Graham Parker, Madness, The Specials, J Geils and others, including many hometown rockers.

Even local public television and Walker Art Center (a catalyst for showcasing "underground" or emerging artists, locally and nationally) got in the act. PBS producers Kathi Riley and Marian Moore (who went on to produce the popular, all-female ensemble Women Who Cook) presented a weekly show highlighting the music scene with many local and international acts of all stripes, called *NightTimes Variety*. The Walker's Tim Carr (another former rock critic who went on to work in A&R at the major labels) mounted the country's first two-day new wave festival in September 1979 at the University of Minnesota's field house called Marathon 80, mixing international and Minnesota bands. Devo played as "Dove," a group of born-again evangelists, in a gospel spoof that floored both fans and disbelievers.

The Commandos and others played "M-80," and were one of the earliest local acts that Statler committed to tape and history. He also shot the vid for "Stop" by The Flamin' Oh's at the Landmark Center (dressing the quartet like classical blokes in natty tuxedos). Formerly Flamingo, the Oh's, ironically, weren't on Twin/Tone and were a group that should have enjoyed a huge commercial success based on their scalding live sets and scads of timeless, well-crafted songs like "I'm a Gun" and "I Remember Romance." They released a reunion album (*Long Live the King*) of new material in 2005.

Ditto for Curtiss A and The Suburbs. A (for Almsted, who every year since John Lennon's death in 1980 has honored him on Dec. 8 at First Avenue with a must-see night of Lennon songs) never seemed like he wanted to leave town for anything, let alone something like a rock career or success. Nonetheless, the "Dean of Scream" remains one of Minnesota's all-time greatest rock singers.

The Suburbs, a well-dressed combo from the western 'burbs, featured the accomplished and often romantic songwriter and keyboard player Chan Poling and his manic foil and guitarist Beej Chaney along with their rhythm section of Michael Halliday and Hugo Klaers, with guitarist Bruce Allen. They issued their two-disc masterpiece in 1981 called *Credit in Heaven*, consistently made good records after that and played pogo-happy live gigs (and some knock-out reunion shows 20-some years later). But through circumstances beyond their control, or other factors, management, the tragic unsolved death of the Oh's keyboard player, Joseph Behrend, or the simple rolling and tumbling of the dice – it never happened on the next level.

To a measured degree, it did happen for other bands from the period, among them the always-popular Limited Warranty and Sussman Lawrence. For all their musical chops, an album for Atlantic Records and a single "Victory Line" that shot to 64 on *Billboard*, Warranty might still be best known for winning *Star Search* (with Ed McMahan), a popular precursor to the staged "reality" shows like *American Idol*. "We dubbed it 'Scar Search,' since nobody ever went anywhere after they won," laughs the band's Paul Hartwig. Like some of his bandmates and the guys in Sussman Lawrence, today Hartwig works here and in Los Angeles composing music for advertising, film and television. He won an Emmy for Gayle Knudson's short film, *Grandfather's Birthday*, which netted 23 awards worldwide.

Although constantly dogged by Twin Cities critics, Sussman Lawrence (and later The Peter Himmelman Band) had a big following (especially for its wildly unpredictable live dates) and its expansive pop palette. Himmelman, the band's leader (and Bob Dylan's future son-in-law), had played in Shangoya and soul/R&B singer Alexander O'Neal's band and had exquisite good taste in rock, pop and blues, which informed his best work. *Billboard* accurately pegged the sound of his band as a "cross between Bruce Springsteen and Elvis Costello." He later went on to a strong solo career in New York and LA making records for Island and Epic, doing the music for TV shows such as *Judging Amy* and *Bones* and making a number of well-received children's albums. *Rolling Stone* called his first solo outing (a tribute to his late father), *This Father's Day*, "stunning."

In its day, Sussman Lawrence produced three albums on Deep Shag Records, including an impressive double set called *Pop City* in 1984. By then, that's pretty much how the Twin Cities music scene had evolved – out of the underground and into the wider blue yonder, literally leaving behind a few crucial embers: Oar Folk burned down in 1985 only to be replaced by Treehouse Records in the same spot, now run by Mark Trehus, an occasional writer and big fan of all sorts of music. Trehus recorded everyone from bluesmen Ray and Glover to the next wave of rockers like Cows, TVBC, Funseekers, the Mighty Mofos (the Batson brothers next band), Babes in Toyland, Rifle Sport and others. The CC Club, with its gilded jukebox and the occasional ghosts of rockers past, present and future floating in and out, is still open across the street. ♪

Curtiss A in the early-'80s: Among other musical engagements, "The Dean of Scream" and former Twin/Tone recording artist has been paying homage to John Lennon's work since 1980 with a host of Twin Cities musicians every Dec. 8 at First Avenue.
(photo: Greg Helgeson)

The Flamin' Oh's (formerly Flamingo) don tuxes, greasy kids' stuff and
odd instruments at Landmark Center for the making of their rock video, "Stop,"
shot by pioneering pre-MTV music filmmaker Chuck Statler.
(photo: Greg Helgeson)

Sign of the times: A rock-packed week of dates at the fabled Longhorn Bar that ran in the
*Twin Cities Reader* when The Suburbs were on the ascent.

The Suburbs: Hugo Klaers, Chan Polling, Bruce Allen, Michael Halliday and Beej Chaney.
Like many of their peers in the new wave era, The Suburbs never got the break to push them
beyond the adoring fan base locally.
(photo: courtesy Polygram Records)

The world's biggest rock fan, Peter Jesperson (second from left), and David Johansen of The New York
Dolls (with child) hold forth at OarFolk with co-owner Vern Sandeen (far right).
(photo: courtey Peter Jesperson Archives)

Peter Himmelman, who led Sussman Lawrence and his own band, has had an even more successful
solo career living in New York and, later, Los Angeles.
(photo: courtesy Epic Records)

Pioneering rock video/filmmaker Chuck Statler on location with Elvis Costello and The Attractions
in Vancouver for the song, "I Can't Stand Up (for falling down)": His work with influential local and
international bands preceded the dawn of MTV and has been featured recently at places like the
Museum of Modern Art in Manhattan.
(photo: Matt Quast)

Shangoya: The late Peter Nelson (center) from Trinidad was among the first to introduce live reggae and calypso to Minnesota audiences, along with Ipso Facto later.
(photo: Greg Helgeson)

Limited Warranty: The popular winners of *Star Search* (an '80s version of *American Idol*).
Paul Hartwig (left front) went on to win an Emmy for his soundtrack for the internationally
acclaimed short film *Grandfather's Birthday*.
(photo: courtesy Atlantic Records)

Tetes Noires: French for "black heads" – or brunettes – the musically eclectic Tetes were a highly
influential band of women in the local new wave period which was dominated by all-male rock bands.
(photo: courtesy Tete Noires)

# Minnesota's Bar Band Era
## *Big Hair, Billowing Fog and Hard Rock*

The Minnesota music scene that produced its greatest songwriters and most legendary musicians also spawned a slew of aspiring rock groups from the late-'60s through the early-'80s with huge followings. Some even sold millions of records and frequently were better received critically in other Midwest cities like Chicago, Milwaukee and Madison. Often they sported big hairstyles and cranked power chord opuses with industrial-strength bridges and gnashing guitar solos.

Throughout the '70s and into the late-'80s, regular dates at suburban and inner-city clubs packed fans into venues like the Iron Horse, Boyd's on the River, the St. Croix Boom Company, Thumpers and Mirage (next door to Duffy's in Minneapolis) and the ever-popular headbanger's romper room, Ryan's Corner, in downtown St. Paul. The destination showcase ballrooms like The Prom Center on University Avenue of the '50s and early-'60s gave way to the often-smoky spaces for first-class rock gigs at halls like the Labor Temple in Minneapolis and in an abundance of nightclubs in both cities and their suburbs.

The Soma Records era produced decidedly benign rock 'n' roll compared to what followed in that psychedelic period and beyond. At least four major groups – The Litter, Gypsy, Cain and Crow – would momentarily erase the memory of innocent-sounding surf twang and dance band

Chameleon: Remembered for their hard rock sound, revolving drum set and Yanni, second from left, who later went on to global fame as a music composer for film, special events, PBS specials and other milestones.
(photo: Associated Press, inset photo: Greg Helgeson)

tunes. In its place they offered blistering, high-volume songs and full-tilt jams – often with complex musicianship and poetic lyrics – that alternately suggested everything from a good freakout to a heavy meditation on the meaning of it all.

Of course, the opposite sex was often at the eye of the storm, along with equally serious subjects like the Vietnam War, complete with all the day-glow trappings of the counter-culture and its summers of love. Later, groups such as Chameleon, Fairchild, Dare Force, Jesse Brady, Sterling, Berlin, Judd and countless others would draw legions to area watering holes. They played more commercialized rock, pop and metal, each with its own signature, quirks and analog recordings that were produced on vinyl platters, 12-inch licorice discs that today look typically quaint and outmoded.

According to The Litter's web site, there were 12 versions of the band until 2000, with cofounder Dan Rinaldi in every one. Their rare and collectible, late-'60s single "Action Woman" has been widely covered over the years by The Hyptrz, The Replacements, British bands and others. The Litter also had the distinction of being among the first groups to use strobe lights and billowing smoke in the live sets regionally. By the time K-TEL Records later re-issued their essential *Distortions* and *$100 Fine* albums, fog machines were de rigueur and became loveably clichéd effects of the Twin Cities burgeoning rock scene and of the stagecraft for nationally touring rock groups.

The extremely loud and influential Litter was the top draw at Chicago's Electric Theater, where they reportedly cut seven songs in the film *Medium Cool*, only to have their music

supplanted (over their images) with compositions by Frank
Zappa ("The Mothers of Invention"). How loud were they? In
1969 the Theater held a contest to see which band was louder,
The Litter, or Blue Cheer (frothing acid rockers). The Litter
won hands-down, says the band's engrossing site.

A hippie-driven monthly music newspaper called
*InBeat*, published, edited, "most likely typeset" and largely
written by Steve Kaplan, who's now an editor at the edgy
*Law & Politics* magazine, chronicled many of the local bands
in each issue from the mid-'60s to the time of the Monterey
Pop Festival in California. Then well-known photographer
Danny Seymour (who mysteriously disappeared in a boat on
an ocean a few years later and was never found) supplied
photos, including those of national acts like James Brown at
the notorious Flame bar in Minneapolis. Brown actually flew
Kaplan and Seymour to St. Louis after his show that night on
a Leer Jet to do an interview and give them a tour of King
Records, marking an extreme high point in the annals of local
rock journalism. True to the times and spirit in which *InBeat*
existed, the paper folded when its principals failed to return
from the music love fest on coast. But bands like The Litter
– as they said then – "kept on keeping on."

Crow struck with a killer national hit in 1968 with the
single "Evil Woman," lit up by Dave Wagner's commanding
voice and Dave Middlemist's heavy organ churns. The band
featured players who had been in The Rave-Ons, Jokers Wild
and South 40 and got their break when, as South 40, they won
a Des Moines rock contest, sponsored by the National Ballroom Operators Assoc. (!). That inauspicious contest changed

their name and fueled their flight for the next several years until they quickly disbanded in 1971 over contractual record label and related financial issues, although they can still be seen from time to time on area stages like Renegades in Burnsville. During their short but powerful run they played with Blood, Sweat & Tears, Jefferson Airplane, Three Dog Night, Steve Miller Band, Bo Diddley, Steppenwolf, Eric Burdon & War, Janis Joplin (three separate times) and Iron Butterfly, according to their nostalgic web site history.

With an urge to make it nationally, The Underbeats left Minnesota to do some California dreamin', also in '68. The former Soma Records group became the house band at the legendary Whiskey A-Go-Go club on Hollywood's Sunset Strip, which led to the metamorphosis of the beloved hometown rockers into the band Gypsy, with its songwriting ace, the late Rico Rosenbaum (who died in '79 at age 36), and its tasty guitarists James Walsh and Jim Johnson. Johnson would stay in LA for almost 30 years, writing for the Fifth Dimension, Ray Charles and others, while placing songs in several movies like *Slapshot*.

Like Crow, Gypsy's journey was short-lived, but their legacy endured. They cut a self-titled double album for Metromedia Records, with its classic album art cover, did a followup LP *In the Garden* in '71 and subsequently made two less successful discs for RCA. The band played the major rock palaces like Winterland, the Fillmore East and West and later featured such seasoned studio musicians as Willie Weeks in the group, who later worked with George Harrison and other notable musicians. Both of Gypsy's venerable axemen can still be heard in the area bars today.

With a stunning five-octave range and a rep for wild,
wild stage shows, Jiggs Lee remains one of the finest rock
singers and performers in Minnesota's storied rock 'n' roll
chronicles. Lee's band, Cain, with Dave Elmeer, Lloyd Forsberg
and Kevin DeRemer (who later married Melissa Manchester),
blew out a bad-boy combination of pile-drivin' rock, blooze and
early metal. Unfortunately, Jiggs' antics were often at his own
expense as he became a poster boy of the period – and later
also one as a survivor.

"I spent 27 years of my life onstage, sometimes as
the village idiot and as a cheerleader for excessive drink-
ing," he admitted in the news release for *Jiggs Lee*, his much-
welcomed comeback CD in 2003. The new disc with an
unreleased Cain tune also proudly celebrated his 10 years of
sobriety. The album came out just as there was renewed inter-
est in Cain, especially its *Pound of Flesh* album, collectible for
its '70s classic rock sound and notorious also for its graphic
cover art – an open can spilling out fresh renderings from
a butcher shop, "a concept from the ASI Records marketing department run amok," Lee laughed. Today the original
album is widely collectible, especially in Scandinavia. Monster
Records in Texas re-released it in 2003.

Lee's hard rock career crossed paths with many
notable figures, including Joe Soucherey, the *Pioneer Press*
columnist and radio talk show celebrity: The King of Garage
Logic was the drummer in an early-'60s band with Lee, The
Bananas. Jiggs' friendships with members of Cheap Trick,
Styx, Kansas other rock mainstays of '70s rock radio were
tightly forged while Cain worked the unforgiving Chicago

and Midwestern club scene, sometimes playing from 9 p.m. to 5 a.m on Rush Street. According to Jiggs, at 2:30 in the morning, clubs in these cities would often turn into jam sessions with whoever might be in the crowd that night: Fleetwood Mac, Iron Butterfly, Spencer Davis, Todd Rundgren, Mott the Hoople and others. In his post-Cain days, Lee slipped into the '70s cover band Fragile for what seemed like "a simple, low-level club gig....It lasted 12 years and blew up into a major showcase group in Twin Cities rock clubs."

Mention the band Chameleon, and most people will remember them for two things during their 1970s history: First, Yanni, their Greek keyboard player, who went on to have a highly successful solo career writing neo-classical-new age-like music (or "contemporary instrumental" as he calls it in his autobiography) for film and television (and a long relationship with actress Linda Evans). Today he has a worldwide fan base and many outstanding achievements too numerous to list here.

Second, people remember the crazy Rube Goldberg drum kit that accomplished drummer Charlie Adams sported during Chameleon's live shows. It not only rotated 360 degrees but flipped upside down, with Adams pounding away the whole time, never missing a beat (even in the fog), even during the roar from the crowd – including those who later caught him twirling on MTV. It was great rock 'n' roll shtick. But the band made four independent and well-received albums; they charted on *Billboard*; and became Miller Beer's sponsored rock band for a year-long tour of the country.

Adams, who is now a Nashville cat and was trained by Marv Dahlgren, principal percussionist for the Minnesota

Symphony, moved first to LA with Yanni, where together they made nine CDs, on which Adams played and wrote percussion and drums and did drum programming. He also collaborated with Yanni on various movie soundtracks. According to Adams' web site, their music has also been used extensively by all of the major television networks' sports and news programming.

Their video with the rest of Yanni's musical entourage, *Live At The Acropolis*, went platinum and played on PBS. Dugan McNeill, the hot guitarist in the band, later recorded as a solo artist for Polygram Records, and since has produced a host of famous bands and singers, while also serving on the faculty at the Twin Cities premier school of rock, IPR (the Institute of Production and Recording). His wife, Pamela MacNeill, also works at IPR and likewise has a successful music career, including collaborations with Yanni (along with her husband). She recorded her debut album in 1999, *2 Sides to Every Sky*, and donated 100 percent of profits from the disc to the United Way, which gained her airplay and touring exposure in 50 cities. MacNeill has also sung backup for and toured with pop star Rick Astley.

The much-loved Fairchild band may have had one of the longest runs of all the hard- and pop-rock combos during the era of poofy hair and dry ice nights. They played from 1970 to 1986, enjoying a broad fan base – and rare radio play in regular rotation on KQRS and other AOR channels for their song, "Do You Hear the Call?" off their first album in 1978, *Fairchild*. It was produced by Steven Greenberg, Reid Mclean and Marsh Edelstein. In 1980 they made the *Shadow-*

*land* album, which sold around 10,000 copies and fueled their regular club appearances throughout the Midwest.

Tom Riopelle, guitarist and songwriter, says the band tended to play the popular commercial covers of the day like Journey and Styx, but after *Shadowland* – and the rise in power pop groups of the early-'80s – the band penned and performed almost all-original material. He says he wrote for the band's decidedly commercial strengths, which well-suited their last singer, Brian Kinney. Kinney proved to be a natural entertainer, rock front man and versatile rock and pop vocalist who would later front Rupert's Orchestra and other bands in the area. Besides being the group's main writer, Riopelle had the distinction of playing the big hook on the "Funkytown" recording ("the 'Satisfaction' of the disco era," as he called it).

Later, Fairchild managed more airplay for "Only You" from their self-titled Gold Mountain/A&M debut album in 1985, which instantly looked like it might help break them nationally. They had a sweet, five-year, multi-album deal (almost unheard of at the time unless you were Prince) with the new label run by music veteran Danny Goldberg. But the often-cruel fates of the music business dictated otherwise.

Roughly a year later, Gold Mountain suddenly ended its relationship with A&M and shut down the band's opportunities there, the cord on the fog machine yanked hard from its socket. By then, a new generation of Twin Cities rockers was backstage – or onstage – across town, and the Purple Reign had already begun. And with little notice, the glorious era of analog recording – plus the old model of record distribution piloted early on by The Heilicher Brothers – was ever so slowly slipping into the twilight, as the bar bands played on. ♪

The Litter with founders Bill Strandlof and Dan Rinaldi: Their timeless song "Action Woman" has been covered by everyone from The Replacements to UK rock bands. (photo: courtesy Timothy D. Kehr Collection)

Crow scored nationally with "Evil Woman," but by 1971, the band's big flight was over even though they still play occasionally today in the clubs. (photo: Greg Helgeson)

Cain and its famous 1970s rock album cover, *A Pound of Flesh*.
(photos: courtesy of Cain)

Still rockin': Jiggs Lee today, the man with the five-octave range.
(photo: courtesy Jiggs Lee)

A mainstay of the bar band scene, Fairchild later got its shot with Gold Mountain Records
and rare airplay on KQRS and other area radio stations.
(photo: courtesy of Fairchild)

# The Replacements and Husker Du
## The Post-New Wave Era in Minnesota Music

O ne of their rehearsal spaces looked like a cyclone closet. Stuff everywhere – cups, broken guitar strings, beer cans, take-out food containers, a wasted shirt here, bunch of newspapers over there by the drum kit. Truly underground, The Replacements' cell looked like almost all the others one floor below in what was then known as Metro Studios over on North Third Street in downtown Minne, a catacomb for bands of all sorts trying to "make it." Whatever that was.

But when Paul Westerberg, Chris Mars and the brothers Stinson, Tommy and Bob rose from that dungeon of dreams on North Third to play or record, heads turned and tongues wagged. Of all the rock music that Minnesota pumped out of the lake state, the Mats, as they were soon nicknamed, might be the most legendary. And perhaps the most influential, laying the land mines for the Seattle scene that exploded Nirvana and who knows how many other groups since then who want to suffer, sneer at and salute their world while knockin' the sense out of it.

The Replacements shunned all of the trappings of wanting to be successful, seldom playing the game required to sell millions of records (although their TV appearance on *Saturday Night Live* is still talked about). Sire/Warner Bros. Records A&R guy Michael Hill, whose label later signed the band, told *Magnet* magazine in July-August 2005 issue, "At the same time they seemed to crave the very success they mocked.

Paul Westerberg from The Replacements: After Dylan, the most influential rock songwriter from Minnesota.
(photo: Greg Helgeson)

They wanted you to pick up the tab, but they'd kick you in the ass while you were paying the bill."

According to the Wikipedia, the "Mats scored heavily with critics through the years if not connecting with the masses: "Like its predecessor, *Let It Be*, *Tim* is one of the most acclaimed albums of its era. *Tim* placed 136th on *Rolling Stone's* 2003 list of the 500 greatest albums of all time, and it ranked No. 4 in the *Associated Press* list of the Top 99 albums of 1985-1995. Along with *Let It Be*, it is one of two Replacements albums to receive the full five stars from the *All Music Guide*."

The band's live shows were guaranteed wild cards. Would they be too plowed to play, brilliantly on, or would they sloppily do two sets worth of covers and not care like they did at CBGBs in New York after being on the cover of the *Village Voice* in December '84?

"Every A&R person in New York was present at CBs while they joyously flushed the set down the toilet, doing nothing but fractions of other people's songs," recalls Peter Jesperson, who discovered them for Twin/Tone Records and later went on to (sorta) "manage" them. Today their records still pack that indescribable *uber* kick you get in all seven chakras every time a laser or needle falls on a timeless rock 'n' roll record.

Looking back, The Replacements were defined early by the punk and indie rock period (1979-1984) in which they were together (they eventually broke up in 1991) despite the fact that Westerberg was a huge Faces fan, who also dug Roger Miller and Ricky Nelson. But when it was all over and an entire generation of indie acts had been signed to major

labels, including them, they often defined those years with
their ballsy anti-anthems like "Bastards of Young," "Kids
Don't Follow" and others. They also delivered well-deserved
cynicism in memorable jabs like "Seen Your Video," "Color
Me Impressed" and "Waitress in the Sky" along with the
despairing pain of "Here Comes A Regular" and "Swingin'
Party." Westerberg's darker stuff was miraculously balanced by
his innocent-sounding "Kiss Me on the Bus," "Alex Chilton"
and "Can't Hardly Wait," proof that he could write catchy,
lyrical pop songs as easily as punky paeans to teenage angst,
love relationships and the machinations of scenesters. Plus,
you won't find a prettier ditty about our supersized gerbil silos
than the one he penned called "Skyway."

By now their story is as worn as the flannel flag that
the flew over the band's fort: Tommy was 12 when the band
formed. Today he's in Guns 'N Roses and Soul Asylum and
has a couple of solo albums under his own belt. Twin/Tone
Records signed them on the strengths of a basement-made
cassette they dropped off for Jesperson at Oar Folkjokeopus.
Chris Mars, the quiet guy voted most likely never to be a
Replacements drummer, held forth on the skins, sharing
what *City Pages* writer Jim Walsh described in *Magnet* as a
Catholic school boy bond with Westerberg. Today Mars' crit-
cally acclaimed paintings, surreal and macabre, practically
overshadow his role in the band and his own solo albums.
Drummer Steve Foley later replaced him to ride out the
storm to the end.

Tommy's brother Bob occasionally donned a dress
to play live, but his buzzsaw guitar leads could drop wasps

from their nests. Still, years of drug use and alcohol caught him up in a swift current, sweeping him out of the group in 1986 that he had founded and copping him a tragically early death at 36 in 1995. Well-known guitarist and solo artist Slim Dunlap, whose musical vocabulary ranged from country and rockabilly to hard rock and blues, stepped in to round out the final years. But their tale still wages. Columnist Jim Walsh is writing an oral history of the Mats, and their exploits are already featured in *Our Band Could Be Your Life: Scenes from the American Indie Underground, 1981-1991* by New York writer Michael Azerrad.

Westerberg, whom filmmaker Cameron Crowe once said succeeded better at telling the trials and troubles of the young in one song than in any movie he's made on the subject, has gone on to a prolific and high-profile solo career, cranking out CDs and occasionally touring like a man in a hurry to get it all said and done. One wag compared his post-Replacements output to that of Prince. Late in 2005, while completing a soundtrack for the hit Sony Pictures movie *Open Season*, he teamed up with Tommy and Mars (who did not drum but sang backup vocals) to pen two new songs for the 2006 Rhino Records Best of The Replacements compilation, characteristically called *Don't You Know Who I Think I Was*.

All kidding aside, one of *Open Season*'s most poignant cuts (lifted from his *Eventually* solo album) is allegedly written for Bob Stinson and shows that the wisdom of ages comes even to the wilder rock sages: "A good day is any day that you're alive/Yes a good day is any day that you're alive." And in a sure sign that the old young man's band's place is secure in the league of rock superanitheroes, a contemp indie punk label, 1-2-3-GO! Records, is releasing in the fall of 2006 a 23-song/band tribute to the group titled *We'll Inherit the Earth*, according to one of the many fan web sites, colormeimpressed. com. There are already three other Mats CD homages, one from Athens, GA., one from LA and an Australian collection from '99 entitled *I'm In Love With That Song* that Jesperson says "is worth seeking, it's really a knockout!"

As for the long-rumored Replacements Twin/Tone-Sire Records album reissues, all eight are scheduled to be released simultaneously with bonus tracks early in 2007, followed by a box set later that year or in early -'08. Can a Rock 'n' Roll Hall of Fame induction be far behind?

If the Mats flirted with punk as merely one genre to work in, their across-the-bar rivals, Husker Du, squatted on it with a vengeance. A powerful thrashing trio led by then Macalaster student and guitarist Bob Mould, drummer Grant Hart and bass player Greg Norton with his wide handlebar moustache, Husker Du was a prototypical punk primitive band back in the day. Formed around 1979, their music quickly evolved in the rough course of 10 years together. Hart's soft melodic side, Mould's seething anger, and their ability to shade even their hardest sounds with other musical flourishes that traveled well out of bounds for most hardcore bands, put Husker Du in a class by themselves. Innocently named after a popular board game (which means "Do you remember?" in Danish and Norwegian), their sound was their fury and their fury was their sound.

With Mould screeching indecipherable lyrics until the veins in his neck and the ears of the audience popped, and his way loud axe droning for a kill, the group often trailed one song after another with barely a break during live sets at the Seventh Street Entry and other dives. Like seeing some exotic ritual, it was mesmerizing to watch, deafening to hear. Soon embraced by college radio and hardcore punk fans nationally, the Huskers sonic-flash-pot shows and Mould and Hart's entangled songwriting started winning over critics and talent scouts at labels.

After putting out a couple cool singles and EPs on Reflex Records, a local label from another Oar Folkjokeopus record clerk, Terry Katzman, and then records on the big alt rock label SST where label mates included The Minutemen, Meat Puppets and other American punk pathfinders, Warner Bros. signed Husker Du in 1986. But not before they had cut what many considered to be their piece d'resistance, the double album *Zen Aracde*, which *Rolling Stone* called a classic, right up there with the Stones' *Exile on Main Street* and The Clash's *London Calling*.

Perhaps one of the more complex groups in terms of band dynamics, personal demons and countervailing personalities, the Huskers also grappled with drug issues. Hart and Mould, who both later came out, seemed to be chaotically cojoined like Siamese twins in their songwriting and personal interactions with each other, leaving Norton the proverbial straight guy. The two never really were able to separate or quell the embattled energies that drove the group, but, as William Blake says, without contraries there is no progression.

As they got more popular, their influence reached overseas. Eventually a young manager they hired named David Savoy around the time of the Warner Bros. deal, took his life, casting yet another pall over their affairs. Prior to that, in 1985 they covered "Love Is All Around," the theme song to the *Mary Tyler Moore Show*, as a kind, if ironic, nod to their hometown and the album *New Day Rising*. The title track's repetitive "new day rising" line sounds both meditative and menacing – and full of the band's potential.

Upon the inevitable breakup in 1988, after eight total albums and a handful of singles, Hart formed Nova Mob, and Mould went to play in his new band Sugar, and then forged a solid solo career until the present. As for the band's bass player, he still wears the big handlebar moustache and in late summer of 2006, teamed up with a couple of Happy Apple jazz pals and a New York keyboardist in the group Gang Font, featuring Interloper, back in the old 7th Street Entry. But normally Norton today is a chef who owns and operates a restaurant in Red Wing called The Nortons with his wife. It's far from the madding trio that fueled the next generation of rockers with an unforgettable power angst. And yet some- where in the distance, the ripped chords of the Huskers are still bouncing around the stratosphere and giving a bunch of somebodys an idea to form a band. ♪

Husker Du: Hardcore punk trio thrashes it out at the 7th Street Entry, early in its
jagged evolution to greatness with records like *Zen Arcade*.
(photo: Greg Helgeson)

The Replacements (left to right): Chris Mars, Tommy Stinson, Bob Stinson, Paul Westerberg.
Their now-legendary live sets were guaranteed wild cards.
(photo: Greg Helgeson)

## The "Minnesota" Song by Northern Light
### *March through Summer 1975*

Twin Cities musicians David Sandler and Spencer Peterson (friends of the Beach Boys' Brian Wilson) wrote this song in 1974 and convinced John Sebastian to play it on KDWB in the Twin Cities. The tune, loon calls included, is a surf sound take on one who leaves Minnesota for "Californiay" but wants to return to the "lakes and the trees back ho-e-o-e-ome." The song charted nationally and the band toured with Kansas in the summer of 1975.

Northern Light in the mid-'70s (from left) Don Beckwith, David Sandler, Bud Phillips, Steve Hough, Spencer Peterson. Other band members are Nick Raths and Gary Lopac. Hear a sample of "Minnesota" from the *49th Parallel* CD at www.glacierdisc.com
(photo: coutesy Northern Light)

---

## Minnesota Music Night Clubs and Concert Halls
### *(Where We Saw the Bands)*

**The Opera House**, Magoo's, **Lucky's**, Jay's Longhorn, **Bronco Bar**, Carlton Celebrity Room, **The Labor Temple**, Zorbaz, **The Press (St. Cloud)**, Williams Pub (Duluth), **The Oz**, The Barn (Alexandria), **The Red Carpet (St. Cloud)**, The Depot, **Uncle Sam's**, First Avenue, **7th St. Entry**, Duffy's, **The Cove (Superior)**, Cabooze, **St. Croix Boom Co.**, The New Munich and ALL the Ballrooms, **Big Reggies' Danceland**, The 5th Dimension (Mankato), **Bimbo's**, The Cascade 9, **The Union Bar, Pudges**, The State Fair Teen Fair, **The Purple Barn**, The Hideaway, **Doc Holliday's**, Libation Station, **any bowling alley**, The Chain Link, **The Terp and Tower in Austin**, Schliefs Little City, **The 400 Bar**, The Rusty Nail, **the 494 Strip**, Rupert's, **The Leaning Post**, Classic Motor Co., **Boyd's on The River**, Dania Hall, **7th Street Rec.**, The Triangle, **Roller Garden**, The Whole Coffeehouse, **The Brass Phoenix**, The Grotto (Winona)

Timothy D. Kehr

A veteran music critic and producer, Timothy D. Kehr produced "Liar Liar" for the Castaways and hand-picked The Litter. Playing a critical role in Minnesota music, Kehr's other connections include Crow, Northern Light, Buddy Holly, The Rolling Stones and major record labels like Colombia and Epic. Kehr has also hosted his own late-night TV show in the Twin Cities. He was named a top executive by *Billboard*, holds gold records and is a voting member of the Grammys. Kehr is also a member of the Minnesota and Iowa Music Halls of Fame.

Big Reggie from Danceland with the famous Brits. The only promoter to lose money on both The Beatles and The Rolling Stones! (photo: courtesy of the late Ray "Reggie" Colihan)

Tom Tourville

A Fairmont native, Tourville has authored 15 books on Midwest Music including *Minnesota Rocked! The 1960s*. Tom writes: "From Mankato to Moorhead, hundreds of garage bands defined the Minnesota Sound. In Mankato, the Gestures, in Duluth, The Titans, and statewide, bands like The Messengers, The Rogues and The Epicureans were budding rock stars. Being there in the '60s was like having an all-access pass to the music." Tourville currently resides in Iowa, still chronicling and contributing to music collections.

Gary Come Home!

Gary Puckett, who led the Union Gap in the '60s and '70s, was born in October of 1942 in Hibbing, just a year and a half after Bob Dylan. Puckett left Minnesota as a youth, later forming the The Union Gap and charting with "Woman Woman," "Young Girl," "Lady Willpower" and "Over You" among other hits. Puckett, who continues to tour, returns to his home state occasionally, and in recent years, has played at the Minnesota State Fair with his band.
(photo: courtesy GP Music)

Michael Johnson was born in Denver and traveled the world before landing in the Chad Mitchell trio in the '60s, playing alongside another with Minnesota connections: John Denver. Johnson moved to Minneapolis in the '70s, from where he reached the charts with "Bluer than Blue" and "This Night Won't Last Forever," among others. Johnson records and tours currently out of Nashville with his brand of country/folk and soft rock music.
(photo: courtesy Michael Johnson Music)

## About the Author

### Martin Keller

Martin Keller has worked as a journalist, screenplay writer, pop culture critic and public relations professional over the past 30 years. His work has appeared in  *Leaders, Rolling Stone, Billboard, The Washington Post, The Boston Globe, Final Frontier, Utne Reader* and other national publications. Keller covered the arts, business and cultural affairs for several Twin Cities publications such as *The Journal of Law & Politics, Corporate Report, CityBusiness, Minnesota Monthly, The Star Tribune, The Pioneer Press, City Pages* and *The Twin Cities Reader*. He has appeared on such broadcast programs as NBC's "Today Show," CBS' "48 Hours," Public Television and Minnesota Public Radio. Awards include a prestigious Minnesota Film Fund Award from the McKnight Foundation and Blockbuster Video and an International Association of Business Communicators Award for Excellence. Keller has also co-written four screenplays and developed two television pilots. He currently practices public relations with his own company, Media Savant Communications Co.

---

# Coming Up

## More Minnesota Music!

Look for more of your favorite Minnesota musicmakers when The Minnesota Series publishes an encore Music book:

**Go inside the Purple Reign of Prince**, and learn more about the legendary Flyte Tyme team of Jimmy Jam and Terry Lewis.

**Take a look back at Minnesota's jazz**, country and bluegrass scenes.

**Read about The Jayhawks** and Soul Asylum, and bluesman Jonny Lang.

**Discover northern Minnesota's** finest musicmakers.

**Stay tuned for this all-night jam session!**

**But first, see what's next in the Minnesota Series:**

## Media Tales

In our next book:

**Read about Minnesota television** with stories on KSTP, WTCN, Dave Moore, Barry ZeVan, Steve and Sharon, Ron and Paul Majors, plus children's favorites Casey, Clancy, Carmen and more. **We'll cover radio and personalities** past and present with stories about WDGY, KDWB, U100, WCCO, KFAN, Rob Sherwood, True Don Bleu, Boone and Erickson, Knapp and Donuts, Steve Cannon, The KQRS Morning Show, Garrison Keillor and more.

**Read about Minnesota newspapers and magazines** and the personalities who made them great.

**Media Tales will be packed with rare photographs.** ... From Duluth to Austin, The Minnesota Series' Media Tales covers it all!

Above: Prince (photo: Associated Press), Dave Moore (photo: Pavek Museum).